# THE
# MALDIVES

Kirsten Ellis, a New Zealander, is the author of a number of travel guides. After seven years residence in Hong Kong and India, she is now based in Europe.

# THE
# MALDIVES

Kirsten Ellis

Photography by Dominic Sansoni

Distribution in the United Kingdom, Ireland, Europe and certain
Commonwealth countries by Hodder & Stoughton, Mill Road, Dunton
Green, Sevenoaks, Kent TW13 2YA

British Library Cataloguing-in-Publication Data
A catalogue record for this book is available from the British Library

Editor: Nigel Sitwell
Series Editor: Anna Claridge
Illustrations Editor: Caroline Robertson
Map Design: Bai Yiliang
Design: De•Style Studio

Additional photography: Gillian Ashworth 35, 160, 161

Production House: Twin Age Limited, Hong Kong
Printed in Hong Kong by Sing Cheong Printing Co Ltd

*Leaving the sandbars behind*

# Contents

# Introduction

The Maldives is one of the most attenuated countries in the world, comprising of 1,200 islands in 26 distinct coral atolls in the Indian Ocean. Some 200 of the islands are inhabited, 25 of them with a population of more than 1,000 people. Sixty-nine tourist resorts have been established among four main atolls, and are locally classified as 'uninhabited by Maldivians'. The whole country covers an area of about 90,000 square kilometres (36,000 square miles), but only a fraction of one per cent of this is land, and only a small part of that is habitable.

None of this really bothers the average tourist, who only needs to know one or two things about the country—that it has the most beautiful tropical scenery, graceful coconut palms leaning over crystal-clear lagoons, coral reefs promising great snorkelling and scuba diving, and lots of sunshine.

The Maldives attracts about 220,000 tourists a year, of whom roughly a quarter are Germans, 20 per cent Italians, 9 per cent Japanese, 8 per cent British, and a slightly smaller number of Swedes, Swiss and French. Only a few Americans and Australians make it to these isolated islands. The tourist industry began in 1972 and has consistently appealed to outdoors types, visitors who don't mind the lack of nightlife and who enjoy seclusion. Scuba divers praise the Maldives as a serious rival to the Great Barrier Reef and the Red Sea. Its transparent waters are a comfortable 27°C (81°F) all year round, and shifting currents open up fresh dive sites throughout the year.

Almost all tourists are housed in self-contained resorts, carefully distanced by the wide blue coral seas from the indigenous population. Away from the resorts, it is obvious that geographical and cultural isolation has kept the Maldives in a quirky Graham Greeneland all of its very own, a kind of Islamic paradise, somehow barely connected to the rest of the world. Prisoners who are found guilty of even minor infractions of strict Islamic law are punished by being sent to a remote tropical island for long periods, to serve a sentence of separation from their families. International tourists in search of their idea of paradise, however, willingly pay up to $80–150 a day for basically the same surroundings, self-exile amongst swaying palm trees and starched-white beaches from which they are free to leave, though given the choice most would opt to linger.

Each resort offers its own version of fantasy-isle accommodation ranging from the distressingly plebeian to the sumptuously chic. You can be there for a few weeks without the slightest idea you're just a few degrees north of the equator and an hour from India. As sensory deprivation goes it's pretty much close to heaven; pampered amnesia with an international telephone line instead of roughing it in search of cultural exploration.

*Toddy tapper, Ari Atoll*

The Maldives, where nowhere is more than 15 feet above sea level, is in danger of disappearing altogether if the greenhouse effect takes hold and the ice caps melt. The capital, Malé, is still low-rise, sleepy and slow-moving; every time a jumbo jet thumps down on the runway at nearby Hulule airport, it temporarily towers over most of the buildings in the Maldives. Only 691 cars are registered in all of Malé, plus 4,026 motorbikes and 37,781 bicycles. The one-channel television station broadcasts to around 4,000 registered sets in the evenings, though its range extends only a few miles outside Malé. On the positive side, the Maldives still sees no need for insurance for its car drivers, has no municipal taxes, and no personal or corporate taxation.

The society is conservative, but Maldivians are, quite rightly, quick to stress that their brand of Islam—though strictly enforced—is more pragmatic than fundamentalist. The president wields a lot of power on paper—he won more than 95 per cent of the vote at his third election in 1988—aided by the *Majlis* (Parliament), most of whose members are elected but some of whom are appointed by the president. According to the constitution one candidate at a time is voted for in a referendum.

The religious leaders, the *qazis*, have a major role to play, authorizing marriage contracts and serving in the courts. Early marriages are the norm at around 15 to 16 years of age for girls on outer islands and it is not uncommon for people to marry three or four times. The Maldives holds the distinction of the highest divorce rate of any United Nations member country. In 1988, for example, there were 2,114 marriages and 1,560 divorces. Between the ages of 30 and 40 they occur in almost equal numbers, probably because it is so easy. A man merely has to voice the divorce formula three times for it to be valid, though a woman is obliged to plead her case in court.

Public decorum is enforced by non-uniformed police in Malé and tourists are advised to follow official instructions about the standard of attire expected. Women especially should wear clothing that 'must be made of material which is not see-through or diaphanous; a piece of cloth simply wrapped around the torso is not acceptable or indeed permitted,' says a government tourism leaflet.

It was not always thus. An early seventeenth-century French traveller, François Pyrard de Laval, noted that the Maldivians were an extremely lascivious people much preoccupied with sex, a characteristic that perhaps has only disappeared with tighter Islamic scrutiny. In fact, most modern visitors may find Maldivians hesitant and shy, friendly but reluctant to open up. There appear to be no words for 'please' or 'thank you' in common use, which reinforces the impression of the people being unassuming and visibly unemotional. However, the Maldivian language, known as Dhivehi, does employ multiple levels of courtesy in addressing superiors and strangers, a bit like Japanese but not nearly so profuse. There are special forms of address for the *beyfulu*, strictly descendants of royalty and others whose ancestry is related to the Prophet, but now widened to include important families such as those of the top government leaders and foreign heads of state.

Though the Islamic courts do not impose punishments like the severing of a hand at the wrist for common thievery, the novel idea of banishment is often applied. In 1988 the courts pronounced convictions in 1,224 cases; 806 of the offenders were banished, one third of whom were women. The majority were sent away for one or two years, but two of the women were banished for life. An official survey of police court cases showed that in some years the convictions for conducting an 'illegal coital relationship' were almost a third of the figure for common theft. There's at least one penal island where the instigators of an attempted coup in 1988 are 'incarcerated' under blue skies and coconut palms. Nor is curiosity encouraged despite the country's impressive record of 98 per cent literacy. According to a report in 1990 in the New York Times, President Gayoom clamped down on critical publications and arrested the country's best cartoonist. Now, however, the government has transmuted the media by welcoming constructive criticism, responsible journalism and encouraging the freedom of expression. Young Maldivians who go abroad to benefit from further study facilities, have to guarantee to serve the government on their return for periods of approximately three to 60 months, depending on the length of their absence.

Surrounded on all sides by water, the Maldives' fishing industry is its biggest revenue earner after tourism. The fisheries sector amounted to 15.1 per cent of the GDP (Gross Domestic Product) in 1991 and engages about 22.4 per cent of the labour force. It is the second most important source of foreign exchange. Just under half of fish exports are of skipjack tuna, which the Maldives is now advertising as having been caught using 'dolphin-friendly' methods (ie using a pole and long line with a single hook, net fishing being outlawed), where the crew of an eight-man boat work frantically to catch 500 fish an hour. A new line is sea cucumber, a gelatinous food delicacy prized in Chinese cuisine. The Maldives' other claim to fame is that it has the world's only Coca-Cola factory that uses desalinated water. Other than that piece of unhealthy living, hypertension is unknown and with the communal life-style so well established, no one in the Maldives starves. Inflation is currently at a rate of 14 per cent.

The Maldives officially celebrated its 25th anniversary of nationhood in 1990. The changes during that time have been immense with diseases held in check, literacy made near universal, communications improved and wide-ranging social welfare programmes introduced. Foreign aid from independent agencies, development banks and foreign governments—including generous fraternal help from other Islamic countries like Saudi Arabia—have transformed the country and the expectations of its 215,000 people, a predominantly young population expanding at a rapid 3.5 per cent per year. Still, as the Maldives displayed a GDP growth rate in real terms of around 9 per cent in 1989, the nation's goal of putting a telephone on every inhabited island by the year 2000 looks obtainable.

All in all, the Maldives is a fascinating country, sometimes quixotic and elusive, that deserves more exploration than a few weeks' self-imposed incarceration in a tourist resort allows. This book, I hope, will tempt you to try it.

## Selected Booking Agents in the UK

**Maldive Travel Ltd**, 3 Esher House, 11 Edith Terrace, London SW10 0TH. Tel. 071–352 2246/071–351 9351; fax. 071–351 3382; tlx. 941 3168 MAGIC G. This is the only specialist company and is run by 'The Maldive Lady', Toni de Laroque, whose personal flag of a rampant parrot flies on every island she has visited; she is also the official Maldives government representative for tourism in the UK. Apart from offering package tours, ground arrangements are also organised for those who already have flights but require accommodation, and this company is a specialist in last-minute bookings.

**Asia Voyages**, 230 Slakan Road, Addlestone, Surrey T15 2PH.

*Tombstone carvings*

*Children playing on Thoddu*

**Kuoni Travel Ltd**, Kuoni House, Dorking, Surrey RG5 4AZ. Tel. 0306–740500.

**Elite Vacations**, 98/100 Bessborough Road, Harrow, Middlesex HA1 3DT. Tel. 081–864 9818; fax. 081–426 9178.

**Thomson Worldwide**, Greater London House, Hampstead Road, London NW1 7SD. Tel. 071–387 1900.

**Hayes & Jarvis**, 152 King Street, London W6 0QU. Tel. 081–748 5050.

**Inghams**, 10–18 Putney Hill, London SW15 6AX. Tel. 081–780 2277.

**British Airways Holidays**, Pacific House, Hazlewick Avenue, Three Bridges, West Sussex RH10 1NP. Tel. 0293–611611.

**Club Med**, 106 Brompton Road, London SW6. Tel. 071–225 1066; fax. 071–589 6086.

# Facts for the Traveller

## Getting There

Thanks to the tourist industry, the Maldives is well served by a host of international airlines, supplemented during the peak season (December–March) by regular charter flights, principally from Europe. Hulule International Airport near Malé is the country's only point of international entry. Colombo in Shri Lanka, Trivandrum in India, and Singapore are the main jumping-off points to reach the Maldives for independent travellers.

Scheduled airlines operating to the Maldives include Air Lanka (from Colombo), Indian Airlines (Trivandrum), PIA (Karachi), Emirates Airlines (Dubai) and Singapore Airlines (Singapore). KLM flies to Colombo, where you can continue to Malé by either Air Lanka or Emirates Airlines.

The principal charter operators flying to the Maldives are Sterling Airways with one flight from Copenhagen; LTU and LTS from Düsseldorf and Munich; Balair with two flights a week from Zürich; Condor from Frankfurt, Munich, and Düsseldorf; Alitalia from Rome; Lauda Air from Vienna; Eva Air with two flights a week from Taipei; and Zas Air, an Egyptian airline, with three flights a week from Cairo and Shaja (at present it operates flights between Trivandrum and Malé three times a week). Kuoni has a charter flight once a fortnight direct to Malé from Gatwick Airport on Air 2000.

Overbooking is a recurrent problem on international flights during the peak season. It is essential to reconfirm your booking 72 hours prior to departure. If possible, get your booking confirmation number and a computer printout. Check-in time at the airport for international flights is two hours before scheduled take-off.

## When to Go

The most pleasant time to visit the Maldives is between December and March, usually a time of endlessy sunny days, when the clear calm waters can be seen at their transparent best. However, this is the peak season so book well in advance. It should also be noted that January is the most congested month.

Weather during the low season of late April to early November is not as predictable, but prices at resorts and hotels are usually heavily discounted. The worst time to go is the time of the southwest monsoon, between late April and late October, especially June, when there can be storms and torrential rain. Throughout the year, temperatures range from 24°C to 33°C (75°–87°F) with a fairly high humidity level cooled by sea breezes.

## Visas

Officialdom is remarkably pared down in the Maldives. Until 1978 it was one of the few countries in the world that did not require visitors to show passports on entry. Today, though, a valid passport is essential and a 30-day tourist visa is issued free of charge on arrival at Hulule International Airport. No photographs are necessary. Holders of Israeli passports are not allowed entry.

Few visitors exceed the visa time limit, but an extension of stay can usually be granted for a further three-month period. Do this at the Department of Immigration in the Huravee Building next to the police station in Malé for a fee of Rf300. Anyone arriving without a resort booking must have at least $10 a day for their intended stay. You are expected also to have accommodation reserved, but you can do this at the airport Tourist Information counter as you pass through immigration control. However, it is not advisable to do this, particularly in the peak season when beds are at a premium.

## Customs

A strict import ban is imposed on firearms, explosives, narcotic drugs and most industrial poisons or chemicals. Bear in mind that the Maldives is a strict Muslim country. In keeping with Islamic codes, it is illegal to import alcohol, pornography of any kind including nude photographs, magazines or drawings, or any idolatrous statues. Bacon, ham, or pork products also will not be welcomed.

Expect to have the contents of your luggage taken out and displayed in front of a restless queue of fellow tourists by customs officers, a seemingly meticulous and mandatory screening process to which anyone may be subjected at random. Being an Islamic country, alcohol is not welcome and bottles of duty-free wine or spirits will be retained by customs, but can be collected when you leave. (However, drinks can be bought at the resorts.)

## Bed and Airport Taxes

A tax of $6 per person per day is levied on all travellers staying in the Maldives, regardless of whether they stay in a guesthouse or resort, or cruise the blue waters. For those not part of a 'package tour', have US$7 ready for the airport departure tax.

## Time

The Maldives is five hours ahead of GMT. For comparison, it lies in the same time zone as Pakistan, is half an hour behind India and Shri Lanka, and three hours behind Singapore. Many resorts switch their clocks one hour ahead of local time in an effort to make things less stressful when you leave to catch your flight home—which only serves to confuse if you want to listen to your favourite programme on the BBC World Service.

*Unloading the day's catch*

# Climate

The Maldives straddles the equator, which puts it on a par with Kenya, Brazil and Singapore. Its climate is tropical with daytime temperatures ranging from 26° to 33°C (77°–87°F) with about a three-degree drop at night under the open starry skies. There are two monsoon seasons, which are relatively mild due to the country's location on the equator. The northeast monsoon is characterized by gentle, dry winds from November to April. It can bring some heavier rains in September and October, and heavy seas in early November. The southwest monsoon prevails from May to October; in April and May this brings erratic showers with higher winds later in June and July. Conditions are marginally more clement in the south than the north, with fewer storms and slightly less rainfall. Humidity is a constant 75–80 per cent, which is quite bearable. Rainfall averages around 1,900 millimetres (74 inches) annually, largely during the southwest monsoon season, but only picking up in August and running on sometimes into December and even January. The water temperature is a constant 27°C (81°F), even down to a depth of 20 metres (60 feet).

# Health Precautions

Any visitor arriving from areas infected with either cholera or yellow fever must be able to produce an international vaccination certificate. People coming from malaria-infected areas—especially from India and Shri Lanka—will sometimes be asked to give a blood sample, but this is usually only enforced for Indian and Shri Lankan nationals.

The vast majority of visitors to the Maldives will face no health problems, though it's wise to consult your doctor or an official vaccination centre before travelling, to check current requirements and recommendations. Vaccination against tetanus and a gamma globulin injection (against hepatitis) are advisable for all travellers. Malaria has been largely wiped out in the Maldives, but it is still advisable to take a course of antimalarial tablets. There is some evidence that long-term use of antimalarial prophylactics can be damaging to the liver and the retina, so you may wish to smother yourself with mosquito repellent, use mosquito coils, and string up a mosquito net around your bed at night instead.

The odds of falling victim to a mosquito-borne sickness—such as malaria, dengue fever, or filariasis—are quite low, especially if you spend most of your time on a resort island. The risks are greater in Malé which has the highest population density in the Maldives and hence a greater chance of transmission. Diarrhoea and stomach

*Fish market, Malé*

upsets are likely to be the only ailments you will encounter. To avoid them, take simple precautions. Drink only bottled water or water which has been boiled or sterilized. Never take a chance on the water served in Malé's cafés or water drawn from village wells. It may be wise to include some iodine solution or water purification tablets in your personal first aid kit.

If you do have an attack of diarrhoea, the best way to treat it is with a diet of bland foods, such as rice, yoghurt, bananas and bread, with plenty of fluids such as weak tea to flush out your system. If problems persist for more than two days, particularly if accompanied by a fever, consult a doctor as you may be suffering from dysentry, an illness that will require treatment. Emergency medical care in the Maldives is adequate and compares well with isolated parts of India. Evacuation services exist to airlift seriously ill patients away from their resorts, but you should ensure that your medical insurance covers repatriation home in case of dire emergencies. Casualty services are offered at the Central Hospital in Malé.

The plankton in the sea water may cause ear irritation and soreness if you are unused to spending a lot of time in the sea. Antibiotic eardrops will help you to avoid suffering from earache caused by this. Other tips are to take an antibiotic spray for coral cuts, and cream for the sandfly bites you may get while sitting on damp sand, watching the sun go down. Remember that coconuts can fall from the trees, so beware where you sit or sunbathe.

Prevention is better than attempting a cure during your holiday. Increase your non-alcoholic fluid intake by three or four times, protect yourself against the sun (which will be much stronger than you're used to), and use plenty of moisturizing lotions. Don't make massive changes of diet towards fresh fruit or spicy foods. Following these simple guidelines will increase your enjoyment and resistence to illness whilst away from home.

# What to Take

Light clothing is the order of the day everywhere. Remember that there are two standards, one for the almost exclusively western-inhabited resort islands and another for the sleepy Islamic capital of Malé. Wear strictly non-see-through clothes in any situation where the locals can see or bump into you. Even if you confine yourself to your resort, you would be wise to take some long-sleeved shirts and long trousers for covering up until you have got used to the sun.

Do not forget the obvious items like sun screen, a change of bathing costume, and a sunhat. Mosquito repellent, and ointment for cuts and bites, are musts. Many resorts, especially the more expensive ones, sell a wide range of beachwear, much of it very fashionable and imported. In the wet season, bring a light raincoat. A torch and spare batteries are always useful. You can buy film in Malé and the resorts but it's best to bring your own as it is cheaper that way and has probably enjoyed a better shelf life.

# Money

The Maldivian unit of currency is the rufiya, abbreviated as Rf. Each 'rufe' is divided into 100 larees. Currently US$1 equals about Rf10.6. Unless otherwise stated all prices in this book are given in US dollars. There is no black market for the currency and visitors should change their hard currency at the airport when they arrive. Notes come in denominations of 100, 50, 20, ten, five, two and one. There is a Rf1 coin and smaller denominations of 50, 25, ten, five, two and one larees. It's worth bringing your cash in US dollars which are readily traded in the Maldives where resorts, shops and booking agents will accept the greenback in lieu of rufiyas. There are no restrictions when changing cash or travellers' cheques into rufiyas but be warned: you are only allowed to reconvert ten per cent of that amount on departure, and only then if you can produce the original exchange receipts. No bank outside the Maldives will accept rufiyas.

All the major credit cards are accepted in the Maldives, though the only company to have a representative in Malé is American Express (care of Universal Enterprises, 38 Orchid Magu, Malé. Tel. 32–2971; fax. 32–2678).

Most resorts have their own internal systems of accounting, including chits, beads and the like. You can settle such bills in hard currency when you leave. A package tourist can easily spend a fortnight in the Maldives and never handle a single rufiya note.

## Communications

One of the marvels of the Maldives is that instantaneous international direct dialling (IDD) is available from most resorts to anywhere in the world, as well as domestic links within its own scattered islands. The Maldives has one of the most sophisticated telecommunications systems in the region, installed by Dhiraagu, a joint venture between Britain's Cable and Wireless and the Maldivian government. Dhiraagu is building a high-tech earth station on Villingili to replace the present one in Malé and plans to have a telephone on every island by the year 2000. Operator-connected calls come through immediately. As with hotels world-wide, resorts usually add around 10–20 per cent to the cost of each call as a connection charge.

You can make telephone calls and send faxes, telexes, and cables in Malé at the Dhiraagu office, Medhuziyaaraiy Magu, opposite the Islamic Centre, between 7.30 am and 8.00 pm on working days, and 8.00 am and 6.00 pm on public and Government holidays, except Fridays and Muslim holidays. Local calls in Malé can be made through rare public call boxes. Hotels and shopkeepers will lend their telephone if you volunteer the Rf2 charge. Malé numbers are prefixed 31 and 32; North and South Malé Atolls by 44; Ari and Vaavu Atolls by 45; Meemu, Faatu and Dhaalu Atolls by 46; Thaa and Laamu Atolls by 47; Baa and Lhaviyani Atolls by 23.

## News From Home

English language news can be found on one page of both the two Dhivehi daily newspapers, *Haveeru* and *Aafathis*, but whilst in paradise, who wants to know what is happening elsewhere in the world? If you do, TV Maldives broadcasts for five hours daily with a 20-minute English language programme at 9 pm. Compulsive news-gatherers may wish to take their shortwave radios.

# Postal Services

The main post office is on the corner of Chandani Magu and Marine Drive. Officially it is open daily except Fridays, from 7.30 am to 12.45 pm and from 3 pm to 4.45 pm, but is occasionally flexible in its timekeeping. Poste restante services are available. Overseas postcards to anywhere in the world cost Rf5 and take about ten days. The stamps are usually on the large size, so leave plenty of space.

# Electricity

Electricity is 220–240 volts, 50 cycles AC. Plug sockets can vary widely so take an all-purpose adapter. Although the electricity supply in Malé is reasonably reliable, there is no national grid and generator-supplied power on the islands, and even in the capital, can fluctuate. On some islands electricity is restricted to the evening hours only, so take a torch, matches, and candles.

# Business Hours

Government offices are open daily except Fridays, from 7.30 am to 1.30 pm. Banks are open Sunday to Thursday from 9.00 am to 1.00 pm, and on Saturdays from 9.00 to 11.00 am. Shops in Malé open some time between 7.00 am and 8.00 am, and close between 9.00 pm and 11.00 pm. This is feasible because Malé snoozes through a siesta period in the early afternoon, from 1.30 pm until 3 pm, and then again during the main daily prayer time from 6.00 pm to 8.00 pm.

# Etiquette and Understanding

English is spoken widely at a rudimentary level, a tribute to the tourist boom in the last decade and local schooling, so you will be understood both in Malé and on resort islands. However, the lack of any obvious emotion among the Maldivians is a peculiarity many Westerners may find difficult to understand. Not a great deal of fuss is ever made in greeting old friends or celebrating events such as marriages. In fact, the local language of Dhivehi contains no formal greeting, few expressions of concern

(following pages) *Netting fish in the shallows*

and no words whatever for 'please' or 'thank you'. This isn't due to unfriendliness, but stems from habit and self-absorption. Unlike neighbouring India, Maldivians are not outwardly affectionate or curious. And men find it difficult to talk directly to women.

Islamic morals, however, are not to be flouted. The big taboo is physical decency. The law states absolutely 'No Nudism', the fine for which is $1,000. Modesty is required in Malé, and may even be enforced by non-uniformed policemen eager to protect Muslim mores and local civic virtue. However, if you are sensible and bear in mind local sensibilities, you do not need to worry unduly. In general, the Maldivian attitude towards tourists is as pragmatic as that in Indonesia, and certainly not as severe as in Iran. Basically, you can do what you like in your resort, short of naked sunbathing.

Maldivians are not allowed, by law, to sell alcohol, even to tourists in hotel or resort bars. (The government imports Shri Lankans, Indians and Bangladeshis to work as bar staff.) For even this apparently mild transgression, the culprit is likely to have to spend some time on an outer island. Non-practising Muslims, including western women, may venture inside a mosque if suitably attired, except at prayer times.

The Maldivian government likes tourists but earnestly tries to keep the visitors and locals apart. The local community is very small and easily policed by gossip. If you step over the line, everyone will know about it very quickly. It's not worth it.

# Tipping

Resorts and most restaurants and cafés in Malé add the standard ten per cent charge for their services. If you hire a boat, the senior boat boy should be tipped at the end of the trip. If you want to thank anyone, most people will appreciate a present from the duty-free shop, which is off-limits to locals. Airport baggage porters have come to expect a decent tip, about Rf10, for the short walk to the boat pier, though trolleys are now available.

# Shopping

Historically, the Maldives exported tortoiseshell, cowrie shells, mother-of-pearl, black coral and ambergris (a usually sweet-smelling, waxy substance formed in the intestines of sperm whales and used as a fixative in perfumes). Lacquerware boxes made from wood carved on a lathe can also be found, as can *kunnar*, leaves of the screw pine (pandanus) made into strips, then dried and coloured. Tortoiseshell from the hawksbill or other sea turtles is strictly prohibited either for export from the Maldives or importation in the west, as a religious taboo and by law. Collection of turtle eggs is not yet prohibited, but it is best to leave them where they are and not encourage their sale. That leaves stamps, T-shirts, old coins and Maldivian costumes and sharks' jaws.

Despite the Maldives' long history as a trading outpost, there is no point in trying to bargain in most shops. There is little to buy by way of local arts and crafts and some items may even cause problems with customs officials back home if they suspect the tortoiseshell is real.

## Food and Drink

Not surprisingly, the main Maldivian source of protein is fish, mainly tuna and sailfish. Meals consist of a series of variations on the main staples: rice, fish and coconut. Because few islanders or even Malé residents have refrigerators, everything has to be prepared daily. On the islands, perishable food such as milk, butter, meat and fresh vegetables are not generally available unless specially arranged by the management. A local flat bread is prepared by grating coconut flesh and mixing it with flour before baking it on a thin sheet of tin over an open fire. Limes and chillis might be added to the fish to produce a curry that is normal breakfast fare. For the evening meal it's fish again, but this time as a thin soup to soak into the rice. Women on the islands spend much of their time husking imported rice and discarding seeds and stones.

Fish is prepared in many ways. *Hikimas* is fish which is first boiled and then smoked before being left in the sun for several hours; *valomas* is smoked fish; *fihunumas* is a barbecued preparation over which a paste of lime, coconut and chilli is applied before it is cooked over the fire. Fried fish is known as *telulimas*. The variations on this theme are many. *Kandu kukulu* is a fish curry. *Hana kuri* is prepared by frying the fish in spices until it is dry. *Garudiya* fish soup is the Maldivian national dish, made from a pungent treacle-like fish stock and served with rice, lime, onions and green chilli. Concentrated fish stock is *rihakuru*. These dishes are commonly served with roti—plain flour pancakes like Indian chapatis. Maldivians serve fish for virtually every meal, including breakfast, which is usually *mas huni*, a dish made from grated coconut, fish, onion and chilli. The only green vegetable commonly grown on

*T-shirt design*

the islands is *murunga*. Curry leaves abound in the markets with *githeyo mirus*, a particularly virulent miniature capsicum that is a devilish *mirus* indeed! Breadfruit is the commonest carbohydrate in the Maldivian diet, and is usually served fried; *bambukeylu hiti* is a special breadfruit curry. The starchy taro is also common, fried in slices as *ala*. Most exotic is the sweet fruit of the screw pine, which is mixed with bananas, sugar, and grated coconut. Highly popular is *diya hakuru*, a thick honey-like substance prepared from palu toddy, rice and bananas. This is especially popular during the days of Ramadan.

Maldivians like snacks, collectively called *hedhikaa*, though their sweet tooth is mercifully restrained. These are usually accompanied by a plate of betel leaves and lime paste. Favourites are *gulha*, fried fish balls made with an outer coating of rice or wheat flour; *kulhi boakiba*, a spicy fish cake with garlic and chilli; and *bajiya*, a samosa-shaped pastry stuffed with onion, fish, and coconut. A thick pancake made with flour, coconut, and sugar is known as a *folhi* and is often sweet; a *mas fatha fohli* is a smaller version of spicy fish cake, and a *kulhi folhi* is a pancake mixed with a little *rihakuru* fish stock or turtle eggs. *Foni boakiba* is a baked pastry with fried onions on top. *Foni roshi* is a sweet biscuit baked on a griddle like a chapati. Milk cakes are *kiru*, and *kiru sarbat* is a sweet milk drink traditionally taken with tea in tea shops.

The country is not especially rich in fruits though the screw pine's fruit is often sliced and eaten sweet, and three kinds of bananas can be found in the market in Malé, along with a sweet pistachio-like nut.

Unusual foods appear for special occasions. Special sweets and other dishes are enjoyed at Eid-ul-Fitr or Kuda Id the celebrations following Ramadan, the religious fasting month. These are also eaten following Malé circumcision ceremonies.

Though western alcohol is heavily frowned upon, it can be purchased on the tourist islands. The Maldivian toddy is called *raa* and is tapped from the crown of the palm trunk. It's a sweet and quite delicious drink if you can get over the pungent smell. Every village has its *raa vari* or toddy man, who shins up the trees to open their trunks with a machete.

# Getting Around

## FROM THE AIRPORT

Most visitors arrive in the Maldives on prearranged package tours that include the transfer from Hulule International Airport to the prepaid resort island. The type of transport provided depends on the distance, price of the tour and type of resort. Expensive resorts like Cocoa Island and Nika provide a transfer by high-speed launch and some are served by helicopter transfer. More modest resorts use *dhonis*, the traditional wooden all-purpose vessels of Maldivean waters—a lovely way to begin the transition towards total relaxation that most visitors crave. Airport/resort return transfer is included in the package a resort offers its clients; for the Ari zone, you can transfer by speedboat or helicopter if you prefer, but such transfer is not included in the package deal and can work out expensive.

Freer spirits can find their own way on private *dhonis* plying the ten-minute trip between Hulule airport and Malé for around Rf50 (about $5). Arrangements can be made to hire a launch or speedboat for the same purpose at rates negotiable at the pierside.

## IN MALÉ

The capital is little more than a square mile in area, so the most practical way of getting around is to walk. Some cars, motorcycles and bicycles are available for hire. Taxis are also available but must be obtained by calling one of several taxi hire companies, or hailed from outside the Malé Government Hospital where they have a special stand. They do not cruise around town in search of fares. Taxi rates vary from Rf10 to Rf20 depending on the number of passengers and the amount of baggage (Rf5 per piece).

## By AIR

Air transport throughout the archipelago is intermittently provided by Air Maldives, whose two 18-seater Dornier 228s and single Sort Skyvan have scheduled flights five times per week to the distant islands of Gan, calling in twice-weekly at Kadhu and also at South Thiladhunmathi. The Hanimaadhoo Airport was officially opened in October 1992, marking the completion of four airfields in four different regions of the country. The fifth one in Kooddoo is almost ready for operation.

Better-off visitors may wish to make use of Hummingbird Helicopters, a private British company which operates regular transfers from the airport in S61N 24-seater and Mi-8 20-seater helicopters. Hummingbird has nine helipads servicing 40 resorts on Ari, South Malé, North Malé and Lhaviyani Atolls. From the helipad, tourists make the rest of the journey to their resort by speedboat or *dhoni*, which is included in their package price. Fares vary according to distance but are approximately $100 one way. Though usually arranged in advance with the resort, helicopter transport can be personally contracted. It is certainly the most spectacular way to arrive. Passengers are encouraged to move around inside the helicopters during the flight to view the stunning scenery through the large windows. The company also offers 15-minute flights from any one of its nine helipads, giving you superb views of the atolls, lagoons and reefs, and depending on time, of the the island where you are staying, at a price of $66. Full day 'Robinson Crusoe' picnic excursions are also available for $159. Hummingbird will fly you to a deserted island in Ari Atoll, which has a marvellous snorkelling lagoon. While you relax, a delicious buffet is prepared for you and before your return journey to Malé, you are taken to an exclusive resort on Nika Island to freshen up. Contact Hummingbird Helicopters at: MHA Building, 4th Floor, Orchid Magu, Malé (tel. 32–5708/9, 32–5926/7; fax. 32-3161; tlx. 66185 HUMBIRD MF).

## By SEA

Individual travellers who wish to charter a vessel to make their own way to resorts have a choice of traditional wooden *dhonis*, speed-boats and motorized launches. All can be arranged either from representative offices or by haggling with individual boat owners at the pier in Malé. Prices tend to vary from high to very high, which is why this is not a popular option, running at around $150 for a day-long *dhoni* journey and the same for faster transportation.

The most established company for hiring all of the above is ZSS, however there are many others to choose from. Many resorts can make arrangements to hire *dhonis*, speedboats, launches, and even yachts, for pleasure cruises, to explore surrounding islands, or for diving excursions. When island-bound inertia sets in, this is the only way of breaking free in the Maldives. The costs vary with the type of vessel, the crew that accompanies it, and the amount of time you spend away (see Organizing a Boat Cruise, page 36).

It is a long time since the voyage from a remote island to Malé represented a major event in the lives of villagers who had to sail across the archipelago by *dhoni*, often for several weeks. Ferries and *odi*, large wooden cargo boats, now ply between Malé and most inhabited islands throughout the 26 atolls in the Maldives. But they operate on an irregular basis and a non-Dhivehi speaking person will find it very hard to organize transport of this sort. Romantic illusions of being a hardy, adventurous traveller and 'going native' to explore the 'real' Maldives are likely to be shattered by reality. Although a ticket will cost next to nothing, it buys you several days of slow-boat life, chugging along through the surf on a hard bench with a brace of island families, a collection of livestock, and cargoes of smelly breadfruit and dried fish.

Although the past few years have seen some improvements in inter-island ferry and transport services, much remains to be done. Islanders are now demanding a faster mode of transport, and there is talk of hydrofoils and hovercraft soon replacing the old slow ferries. However, this may be wishful thinking and it is likely that transport to most parts of the Maldives will continue at its own slow pace for the foreseeable future.

# Geography and Ecology

The Maldives is a chain of low coral atolls no more than 128 kilometres (80 miles) wide and stretching some 765 kilometres (475 miles) from north to south, running from latitude 7°N to just south of the equator. The country actually forms the central part of the Laccadive–Chagos Ridge, a submerged mountain range which is mostly about 300 metres (985 feet) deep. But the depth increases to more than 1,000 metres (3,280 feet) between the main part of the country and the two southernmost atolls.

The total land area is less than 300 square kilometres (115 square miles)—a tiny fraction of the 90,000 square kilometres within its official territory. The Laccadive, Minicoy, and Amindivi islands to the north—known collectively as Lakshadweep— belong to India, while the Chagos Archipelago to the south forms the British Indian Ocean Territory. The Maldives consists of 1,200 islands together. Only nine are larger than two square kilometres (one square mile), and the biggest, Fuamulak, is just seven kilometres (four miles) at its widest point. Nowhere in the Maldives is more than four metres (15 feet) above mean sea level, so there are no hills or rivers and only one small freshwater lake.

## Atoll Formation

The theory of atoll formation was first expounded by the great English naturalist, Charles Darwin, in 1842. Although he never visited the Maldives, Darwin made a close study of charts and other information about the area and described the differences between barrier and fringing reefs, and explained the creation of isolated atolls. In fact, the English word 'atoll' is derived from the Dhivehi word *atholhu*.

Darwin's revolutionary view was that an atoll is not the coral-encrusted rim of a volcanic crater, as had been thought, but is formed when a small volcanic island, or tip of a mountain peak, gradually subsides into the sea. Coral grows in the warm, shallow water around this island, and as the sea level effectively rises, the coral growth keeps pace. Eventually, the original land disappears beneath the sea, leaving only the doughnut-shaped coral reef, or string of islets, enclosing a central lagoon. The top part of the encircling reef is mostly exposed, and covered with accumulated coral sand and other debris. It has now become an island, or a series of islands, itself. There is a channel through the reef, linking the lagoon with the open sea, which is normally on the leeward side. (There is some argument about whether the land actually sinks, or whether the sea level rises, but this is relatively unimportant as both processes have probably been involved in atoll formation.)

*An idyllic retreat*

In the last year of his life, Darwin expressed the hope that some 'doubly rich millionaire' would confirm his theory by making borings into a coral atoll. In due course, in 1952, the US Atomic Commission undertook just such a series of borings at Eniwetok Atoll, in the Pacific. The coral extended down for 1,220 metres (4,000 feet), and the underlying rock was found to contain fossilized shallow-water creatures, sure evidence that the rock had indeed changed position.

To this day, the atolls of the Maldives are considered the classical examples of coral atoll formation. And the Maldives has the largest true atoll in the world, the Huvadhu, which has a lagoon 112 kilometres (70 miles) in diameter, with a maximum depth of 86 metres (282 feet).

## Malé's Problems

Conservation problems are usually concentrated where humans gather, and Malé is no exception. The key problem is its dwindling water-table of fresh water, a lens of relatively pure water beneath the soil surface that floats upon the denser saltwater held in the porous coral rock on which the city is built. This lens is deeper in the centre than the edges, so it looks like an upside-down bowler hat. This has taken 15,000 years to establish, yet today the total rainfall throughout the entire Maldives archipelago would not be enough to satisfy ten weeks' demand for water in Malé alone.

Since the recharge rate of Malé's aquifer is less than the rate of withdrawal it is now only possible to take freshwater from the centre of the island, supplemented by rooftop rain collection. The freshwater lens takes time to adjust to new levels, so an overpumped well can be fine for several years and then suddenly turn saline. Shallow wells draw the water-table level up even higher in a localised area, as a child's straw sucks up liquid in a glass, distorting the shape of the lens and rendering nearby wells useless. An improved drainage system can mean cleaner streets but it also stops the lens from recharging as easily as before. Salty storm water can be blown over the island, tainting the freshwater further. Malé's lens is now just 120 cm (four feet) below the surface and has a large and unusable brackish zone of contaminated water.

The signs are clear. The deep-rooted trees like breadfruit and mango suffer first. Sewage and pesticides are also a major factor affecting the purity of the source. On outer islands even the ubiquitous coconut is a headache. Coconuts transpire—lose to the atmosphere—a lot of water, around 70–130 litres (15–29 gallons) per tree every day; this compares with human consumption of 20–350 litres (four–76 gallons), a figure that rises to 1,000 (220 gallons) a day in some resorts. As *The Economist* noted in 1988, things are not helped by some Maldivians having two or three baths a day.

The mining of coral for construction purposes is also a worry; removal of the upper two metres (6.6 feet) of shallow reef flats on some islands in North Malé Atoll is still carried out. It's estimated that at current rates of extraction, all the reefs in the North Malé Atoll will be barren by the year 2014, with no recovery during the intervening period. It is no surprise that Maafilaafushi in Lhaviyani Atoll has been selected as the first of the new islands to be colonized to escape Malé's dwindling water supplies and other headaches, and graced with a few extra feet of elevation to escape future inundation.

# Coral

What we think of as coral is actually the external skeleton formed by a community of millions of tiny animals called 'polyps'. These coral polyps are diminutive members of a group of sea creatures, the coelenterates, which include jellyfishes, sea anemones, and sea fans. Snorkellers and divers usually cannot see the coral polyps, partly because they are generally extremely small, but also because they are mostly nocturnal and therefore retracted during the daytime. But if you have the necessary experience, do try a night dive, when you will see them expanded with their tentacles waving gently in the current. The tentacles are armed with stinging cells—nematocysts—which they shoot into passing prey to immobilize them. The prey animals, which are mostly microscopic planktonic creatures, but can also include tiny shrimps and even juvenile fish, are then dragged by the tentacles into the mouth of the polyp.

But the life of the coral polyp has another important aspect, which helps explain its incredible reef-building powers. Inside the tissues of the polyp are symbiotic algae, that is, tiny plants literally 'living together' with the polyp to the mutual advantage of each. The algae use the sun's energy to convert carbon dioxide and water into oxygen and carbohydrates through the process called photosynthesis—and the coral polyp in turn makes good use of this supply of oxygen and extra food.

Besides the so-called 'hard corals', described above, there are also 'soft corals' which are somewhat similar but do not have the massive external skeleton. Instead, they produce a kind of internal skeleton formed in limestone crystals. And some of the soft corals do not have the symbiotic algae of the hard, reef-building corals. One further point is that since algae depend on sunlight, and sunlight is quickly absorbed by seawater, it is rare to find much hard coral growing deeper than 30 metres (100 feet). After that, soft corals, sponges and other organisms that do not depend on the sun's rays start to take over.

The limestone skeleton of the hard coral remains even when the polyps die, and it is this which forms the permanent structure we know as a coral reef. The reefs of the Maldives—and, indeed, they are the life the country—have been constructed over millenia by huge armies of tirelessly energetic coral polyps. Over 200 different species of hard coral are found in the Maldives—which contribute to the diversity of the reef, and of course create an endless variety of habitats for an astonishing range of colourful underwater creatures.

The coral reef as a whole is an immensely complex ecosystem, and the interactions and survival strategies of its inhabitants are endlessly varied—and deeply fascinating for those underwater explorers with the inclination to observe and try to understand their behaviour. Most relationships that are likely to be seen are based on predator-prey interactions. However, there are some other relationships likely to be seen by the diver which are more harmonious. These include the association between clown fishes and potentially lethal anemones, and the mutually beneficial system known as 'cleaning symbiosis'.

Clown fish are brightly coloured fish, usually yellowish with a distinctive blue stripe, that are found hovering above or often half-hidden amongst the venomous tentacles of sea anemones. The fish protects itself from harm by secreting a mucus that disguises its own chemical composition, and at the same time covering itself with the anemone's own mucus. Thus, the anemone is deceived into thinking that the fish is actually part of itself. The benefit to the clown fish of this arrangement is that it is protected by the anemone's tentacles. While the benefit to the anemone is not quite so obvious, it is probable that the anemone is not bothered by potential predators because the presence of the brightly coloured clown fish warns them away.

Swimming around the reef, one can soon spot established 'cleaner stations' where small fish are diligently at work cleaning parasites, dead tissues, and fungus off larger species. The cleaners work over their customers' bodies, including the gill cavities and even inside the mouth, without risk of harm. In fact, the client species often seem to enjoy the experience, and are protective towards the cleaners (who also benefit by getting a meal in the process). Sometimes quite large numbers of bigger fishes will gather at the cleaning stations and it is amusing to see them wait their turn in an orderly fashion.

Besides full-time cleaners (usually species of cleaner wrasse in the Maldives), there are some which only perform this function on a part-time basis and others, such as angelfish and butterflyfish, that do it only while they are juveniles. The cleaners also include invertebrates, especially shrimps.

# Fish Large and Small

Apart from the beauty of the reefs themselves—and many people consider the reefs of the Maldives to be the most beautiful in the world—probably their greatest attraction is the dazzling variety and number of fish that inhabit them.

Firstly the lagoon, which in a typical atoll is surrounded by the reef. A surprising variety of fish can be found here, often at depths of no more than 1.5 metres (five feet). Though the bottom is mainly sandy—not normally a good place to find fish—there are outcroppings of coral that act as magnets for fish. Here you will see damselfish and clown fish, including the blackfooted clown fish which is unique to the area, and juveniles of many other colourful reef species, especially surgeonfish, triggerfish, and wrasse. You may also encounter young whitetip reef sharks in this nursery area. If you have never met a shark before, and are uneasy at the prospect, this is a good place to start, as the youngsters may only measure a metre (three feet) or so, and should allow you to conquer your fears in readiness for the big-time world of the reef itself.

Once outside the lagoon on the seaward side of the protective reef, everything changes. At first you will be awed by the sheer number and diversity of fish. More than 1,000 species have been recorded from the Maldives and the surrounding ocean,

*Emperor angelfish*

## ORGANIZING A BOAT CRUISE

The ultimate way to explore the Maldives is to hire your own luxury yacht-
*dhoni*—a modern cross between a cargo boat and a cabin cruiser. This gives
you total flexibility at all times, the chance to sleep where you choose, and
the opportunity to experience the best aspects of a range of resorts as well
as all the pleasures of relatively calm sea cruising. It is the favoured way to
investigate the best diving spots of the Maldives, but there's no reason why
you shouldn't just cruise around, if you can afford it.

The diving is best between the end of December and April. Charges are
generally calculated per week, where everything bar the drinks—but
including  food—is paid inclusively if not in advance. The cost is about
$65–80 per person per day. Most companies offer 'boat safaris' for a
minimum of seven days, usually aiming for a ten-day cruise but often going
out for up to three weeks. The most popular routes explore Ari Atoll. A
two-week excursion goes as far as Felidhu. Each charter can handle 4–12
people. The luxurious air-conditioned cabins are often beautifully fitted out
with individual bathrooms, wardrobes, and finished in rattan-weave and
dark mahogany wood. Or you can go downmarket for something more
simple with a local look, and perfectly comfortable for a few days' cruising,
with the local crew acting as chef, boat boys, and helmsmen.

The European-run charter companies provide on-board diving
instructors in addition, and the three boats run by a trio of Italian skippers
offer pasta freshly made in the galley. Contact can be made with the
following:

Suntour Maldives.  Giuseppe D'Amato operates a beautiful yacht, the
*Baraa Baru,* which has four cabins suitable for ten people in all, with *en
suite* bathrooms, showers, television and video, and microwave cooking.
This fully equipped diving *dhoni* can be hired out at around $100  per
person per day.

Guido Villa can be contacted through Safari Tours or Agenzia Viaggi
which run deals inclusive of air fare from Italy and transfers with Giorgio
Rosi's company. Most travellers stay for one or two weeks, and most cruises
concentrate on different diving locations.

Agenzia Detours operate four 20-metre (66-foot) and 24-metre (79-foot)
yacht-*dhonis* with five or six cabins each.  Every boat has its own smaller

diving *dhoni*, air compressor, diving tanks, and enough diving equipment for up to 12 people. The Italian chef cooks fresh pasta, catches the fish, and specializes in lobster dishes. Hire charges start at about $120 per person per day, which includes two dives a day for safaris of 9–15 days (minimum of seven days). The company needs ten days' warning to get out of Kaafu to outlying atolls.

The major local operator in the Maldives is ZSS. They offer a diesel-powered *dhoni* for safari at $175 per day, dropping to $40 per person when shared by six or more. A slower boat starts at $130 per day. They also have two types of speedboat: a twin diesel capable of 35 knots at $440 per day with a capacity of ten people; and a smaller one with room for six at $350 for a full day. Yacht-*dhonis* range from $250–350 depending on facilities, inclusive of taxes and meals (charged at $12 per person per day). All boats are in radio contact with base. Diving equipment, including compressor, can be hired at around $75 per day. However there are many other good and reliable operators.

Another alternative is a traditional *dhoni* run by a German called Asim, who married a Maldivian woman and became a Muslim. The boat—which he named *Shadas* after his wife—was used by the Norwegian explorer Thor Heyerdahl during his visits to the Maldives. It is now based at Rihiveli in South Malé Atoll and can be booked via tel. 32–4075 or tlx. 77025 REEFSIDE MF. He does not do diving trips but can advise on them.

It is also possible to book liverboard boats from the UK. The *Magic of the Maldives* is an 80-foot-long, traditional, wooden *dhoni* available for a minimum of six charterers who will be ferried to and from dive sites by an accompanying boat. The *dhoni* has a clear afterdeck for gear storage, deck salon and a galley with a freezer. The six twin-bunk cabins are fan-cooled and have a bathroom with hot and cold water shower attached. The diving is paid for locally. Enquiries to Toni—the Maldive Lady, Maldive Travel Ltd, 3 Esher House, 11 Esher Terrace, London SW10 0TH; tel. 071–352 2246/071–351 9351; fax. 071–251 3382; tlx. 941 3686 MAGIC G.

The *M V Keema* is an 80-foot-long boat, with six twin-berth cabins for 12 people. A 30 foot support vessel provides surface cover, radio communications and oxygen supplies, and equipment is available for video enthusiasts. Contact Maldive Scuba Tours Ltd, 6 Front Street, Mendlesham, Stowmarket, Suffolk IP14 5RY; tel. 0449–766116; fax. 0499–766069.

so it is one of the most species-rich marine areas of the world. With this abundance, you may find your first experience of fish watching bewildering. What you can be sure of is that each dive will be different, bringing new, colourful and sometimes surprising sights. You will want to keep returning again and again.

There are fish of all sizes in the Maldives, from very small ones like the brilliant-coloured fire goby to the massive manta ray and the gigantic humphead wrasse which is the length of a tall man but much heavier, up to 190 kilograms (420 pounds). If you are lucky, you might encounter the largest fish of all, the harmless, plankton-feeding whale shark, which can attain a length of about 12 metres (40 feet) and weigh more than 20 tonnes.

But more likely you will meet those colourful and characteristic reef fish, the angelfish and their close relatives the butterflyfish; the former are mostly seen on their own, while schools of pennant butterflyfish numbering several hundred are not uncommon. There are plenty of large gropers, of which a striking example is the vermilion rock cod, bright red or orange and decorated with a maze of blue spots.

Schools of surgeonfish graze the coral walls of the reef (look for the beautiful powder blue surgeonfish), while large-eyed, nocturnal soldierfish and their cousins the squirrelfish, hang out under ledges. And you can be sure to see jack, snapper, goatfish, fusilier, anthias, coral-crunching parrotfish (you can actually hear them doing it), and a host of others.

There are some special sights to look forward to in the Maldives. Unicornfish are fairly common here, though not so elsewhere. The aptly named cowfish, a member of the boxfish family, has one pair of 'horns' pointing forwards. The large red-faced batfish is a companionable creature, and it is not unusual for a group of them to escort divers while they explore the reef.

*A sprawling coconut palm*

Sharks and turtles—green, loggerhead, leatherback, and especially hawksbill—are relatively common, and an underwater encounter with one of the great amphibians is an outstanding experience. Ungainly on land—and it is only the females who ever return to the beach to lay their eggs—some turtles can reach speeds of 50 kph (31 mph) or more in the sea.

Among other denizens of Maldivian reefs are slow-moving lionfish, beautiful but poisonous—though easy to avoid—and sharp-toothed moray eels poking out of holes in the coral. Although quite harmless unless you harrass them, it is probably wise not to tempt fate by touching a moray eel, as some people do, for it has a grip of steel and you would never be able to pull free if it did choose to bite your arm. Starfish, brittle stars, feather stars, sea urchins, sea cucumbers, sea squirts and hermit crabs are just some of the other life-forms to be seen and enjoyed.

# Land Animals and Birds

Compared with the astonishing richness of the marine life, the terrestrial fauna of the Maldives is very limited, in common with other oceanic islands. Nevertheless, it is quite interesting, though as yet little studied.

Most of the animals have come to the Maldives from India or Shri Lanka, and indeed all of the mammals and reptiles are also found in those two countries except the fruit bat, or flying fox, which is judged to be a distinct Maldivian sub-species. The fruit bat no doubt made its own way to the Maldives, but the other mammals—the black rat, house mouse, and Indian house shrew—were almost certainly introduced by man or came on ships. There are also a few cats and goats, but no dogs as these are not allowed on religious and health grounds.

The reptiles, which may also have been introduced, include two nocturnal house geckos, a colourful agamid lizard that is fairly common on some islands, a skunk, and two nonpoisonous snakes. In addition, there is one species of frog and one toad. Little is known about the invertebrates, but there are nearly 70 species of butterflies.

Birds are more numerous, with more than a hundred different kinds recorded, but only a small proportion of these breed in the islands. The two commonest land birds are the house crow and the koel, a cuckoo that depends on the crow as host for its eggs. These are present on most of the inhabited islands, including Malé, and the resort islands. The crow has increased to pest proportions but no effective method of control has yet been found. The koel by contrast is seldom seen, though its varied and remarkable repertoire of calls (some sound like a girl screaming) are unmistakable.

There is a total absence of small passerine birds. However, the non-indigenous rose-ringed parakeet, bright green with a red bill, is a colourful sight on Malé and nearby islands. The only other land bird likely to be seen is the rather elusive white-breasted waterhen, which nests under low bushes and rank vegetation in the centre of some islands in Mahe Atoll.

Some 13 different herons are found in the Maldives. The commonest is the large grey heron, which stands on the outer reefs of most islands waiting patiently for a suitable meal to swim by. Some of the other herons are thought to be endemic sub-species.

Most numerous are the seabirds, among which are several terns including the graceful fairy tern (though this is confined to Addu Atoll in the south). Two frigate birds breed in the Maldives in small numbers, the great and the lesser; two noddies (which fishermen watch out for as they indicate where the tuna are); Audubon's shearwater; and one of the most elegant of seabirds, the white-tailed tropic bird. It is possible the red-tailed and red-billed tropic birds also breed here.

A number of migrant birds, and others that have been blown off course, visit the Maldives at various time of the year. They include petrels, ducks, shearwaters, various birds of prey, and such birds as whimbrels, plovers and sandpipers.

# Plants

As with the animal life, the Maldives are not rich in terrestrial plant species. Of about 600 species, more than half were probably introduced for food or other human use, such as herbs, in medicine or as ornamental plants or shade trees. Others are common tropical plants that are often found in association with man. It has been estimated that less than 100 species might have colonized the islands before the arrival of man.

Even including all the introductions, the Maldives has far fewer plant species than it has islands, unlike the situation in most tropical island groups. The explantion may be that in the low-lying Maldives there are not many different ecological niches available, and thus only limited possibilities for plant colonization. One very interesting point, which has been noted by Dr Dennis Adams of the Natural History Museum in London, is that most of the common native plants of the Maldives are also found on similar islands in the Pacific, but are rare or absent in between. He suggests that they reached the Maldives from the Pacific, rather than the other way round.

Only five of the Maldivian plants are said to be true endemic species (not found anywhere else), and these are the local varieties of pandanus, or screw pine. The question is still open, however, as it seems unlikely that these trees alone should be endemic, especially as their seeds are very well adapted for oceanic dispersal. Furthermore, the Maldivians themselves do not recognize five kinds of pananus but three, which they identify as small, medium and large.

Of cultivated plants, the visitor may see breadfruit, mango, tamarind, areca nut palms, lime, watermelon, pineapple and banana. Crops include millet, some sorghum, sweet potato, taro, manioc, and Indian arrowroot. Rice is not grown, but substantial quantities are imported.

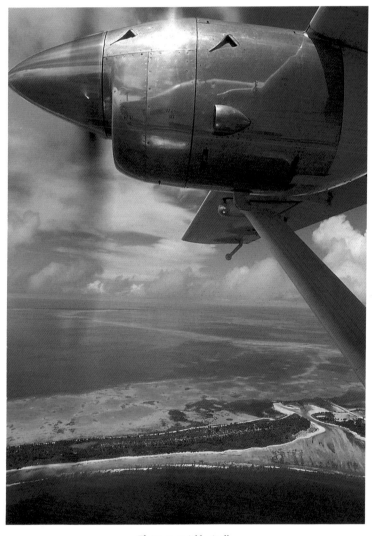

*Flying over Addu Atoll*

# History

Local historians place the first major settlement in the Maldives around the fifth century BC, part of the great Aryan drive southwards and eastwards from the Indus valley in northwestern India. They encountered some people of Dravidian stock already living on the islands, Hindus marooned on the archipelago by shipwreck and circumstance. The Aryans introduced their language *ellu*, a pure form of the Sinhalese spoken in present-day Shri Lanka, and their religion, Buddhism. It is thought that the name 'Maldives' derives from a Sanskrit word *malodheep* meaning garland. Buddhist relics, statuary, carvings, and mounds have been found on at least 60 large islands in the archipelago though no list has been compiled. The eight largest such relics are Nilandhu in Faafu Atoll, Isdu and Fuamulaku in Laamu, Gan in Gaaf Dhall, Kibidhu in Thaa, Thoddu in Alifu, and Landu in Noonu. Landu has one compound with seven stupas of different sizes, including a big one on a raised platform. Archaeological efforts are hampered by a lack of experts to supervise digs. Some Portuguese relics have also been found on Hitadu in Seenu Atoll, Guraidu in Thaa, Kolhufushi in Meemu, Utimu in Haaa-Alifu, and Fuamulaku in Gnaviyani.

## Heyerdahl's Theories

The famous Norwegian anthropologist-explorer, Thor Heyerdahl, had a particular fascination with the Maldives. His curiosity was aroused by pictures sent to him of a statue featuring a man's head with the hair braided in a top knot and ears extending down to his shoulders. The figure was obviously Buddhist in origin, but bore a striking resemblance to figures Heyerdahl had investigated on Easter Island in the Pacific Ocean. Obviously they were not part of Maldivian post-Islamic culture as no representation of the body is allowed in Muslim worship. Where did they come from?

Heyerdahl's conclusion is that the Maldives lay at the crossroads of the great east-west trade routes linking pre-Christian Europe and the Near Eastern civilizations with China and the East Indies. Anyone travelling from east to west would have had to pass through the archipelago. Evidence of this movement, as much as 4,000 years ago, turns up in unlikely places and shows that whoever colonized the Maldives were a civilized people, not simply untutored, shipwrecked sailors. The hawitta mound (like a Buddhist stupa) on Nilandu dates back to about AD 500. Two thousand years earlier, peoples in northwest India and the Indus valley had begun a series of migrations, including south to Shri Lanka and beyond. They were experts in carving solid rock into precision-fitting blocks without masonry, they sculpted lions and bulls, and used the swastika and lotus for decorations, all of which have been found in the Maldives. The phallic stones also unearthed in the Maldives date back to the Indus civilization, the shape prefiguring the representation of Shiva, the important Hindu deity.

As for the cowrie shells found in Scandinavia, as far north as the Arctic Circle, in graves dating back 1,500 years, these seem to have been passed on by Arab traders to nomadic peoples from Finland in exchange for furs. Chinese pottery shards found on the beaches in some southern Maldive islands date from the Sung and Ming dynasties, and are therefore between 450 and 1,000 years old. One fragment, though, has been identified as Neolithic and of a type that ceased to exist about 2,000 BC. Roman coins dating from the time of Christ have also been recorded, and written records from the fourth century mention people calling themselves 'the *divi*' paying homage to a new emperor. The first-century historian Pliny recorded also how the Egyptians made their way to India in order to trade, and used the changeable monsoon winds to bring them back in under a year of travel. The old Maldivian system of counting, using a base of 12 instead of ten, may have been taken from Mesopotamia, site of the old civilizations of Babylon and Sumer.

Records in Shri Lanka talk of a migration west to some coral atolls around 500 BC, at the instigation of a Buddhist seer, so the Sinhalese probably shared the settlement of the Maldives with Hindus from the far north of India 2,500 years ago. The last, and still unsolved mystery, concerns the identity of a group of mound and temple-builders known in Maldivian oral legend as *the Redin*, a white-skinned, brown-haired people with big bones and blue eyes, tall people with long faces who worshipped the statues they made and who came east down the pathway of the sun, sounding uncannily like the pre-Columbians of Mexico and Peru. One such hawitta on Gaaf-Gan appears to be solar-oriented, a square with steps, three lion heads and a relief of a bull.

Perhaps this mystery will never be solved. Unfortunately, almost all the carvings and mounds have been destroyed, either to make new buildings or through religious fanaticism.

## Myth of the Conversion

The Maldives were almost certainly converted to Islam over a period of time. Perhaps as much as a century passed before the belief had spread throughout the archipelago and fully displaced Buddhism. Nonetheless, Maldivians have a strong deliverance myth of this event, which also served to reinforce the righteous power of the new religion over the old superstitions. The Arabic traveller, Ibn Battuta, recorded a legend about two centuries after the twelfth-century conversion that demonstrates the virtue of true Islamic belief.

The legend states that the capital was suffering from the predations of a *rannamari*, a demon of the sea who began plaguing Malé in 1153, threatening to destroy the town unless a virgin was sacrificed every month. The king at the time, one Kalaminja, was forced to accede to these requests until an itinerant Moroccan trader, called Abul Baaketh Yusuf el-Barbary, worked out a way to save them. Disturbed that one of the daughters of the house where he was lodging was next on the rota for sacrifice, Abul decided to take her place. Making his way at night to the temple assigned for the deed, and disguised as a girl, he passed most of the hours of darkness by an open window piously reciting verses from the Koran. When at last he saw the spirit rising from the waters he merely began reciting the verses even louder, causing the demon to squeal with pain and disappear below the waters forever. Not surprisingly, Abul soon persuaded King Kaliminja to convert to the religion that had so amply demonstrated its powers, which the king did, taking the title Sultan Muhammad Ibn Abdullah. He is said to have ruled for 25 years and founded a dynasty, only to disappear suddenly on a pilgrimage to Mecca.

A second version, related in the ancient Maldivian chronicle, the *Tarikh*, tells how Sheik Yusuf Shamsuddin of Tabriz, a renowned and pious man, came to the Maldives and conjured up a jinni as big as the sky on the 12th day of Rabi-ul-Akhir, Anno Hajjirae 548, that is AD 1153, which persuaded everyone from the king down to become Muhammadans.

# Islamic Kingdom

Despite the Maldives' strategic location it has not been the prey of successive foreign powers, possibly because the shallowness of the lagoons and the difficulty of navigation without intimate knowledge of the waters protected the country from interference. Modern historians like to date the Maldives as a defined political identity from the era of the conversion, which would make it the oldest small state in the world outside a brace of anachronisms in Europe.

Life was blissfully event-free until 1495 when a deposed ruler, Sultan Kulu Mohamed ('the black'), turned to the king of the Malabars for assistance in regaining his throne. It is unclear whether this was given the first time this sultan was deposed, for he certainly regained his title at one point only to lose it again. But on this

# The Power of Faith

Trustworthy men among the inhabitants, such as the lawyer Isa al-Yamani, the lawyer and school-master Ali, the Kází Abd Allah, and others, related to me that the people of these islands used to be idolaters, and that there appeared to them every month an evil spirit, one of the Jinn, who came from the direction of the sea. He resembled a ship full of lamps. The custom of the natives, as soon as they perceived him, was to take a young virgin, to adorn her, and to conduct her to the budkhána, that is to say, an idol temple, which was built on the sea-shore and had a window by which she was visible. They left her there during the night and returned in the morning, at which time they were wont to find the young girl dishonoured and dead. Every month they drew lots, and he upon whom the lot fell gave up his daughter. At length arrived among them a Maghrabin Berber, called Abú'l-barakát, who knew by heart the glorious Koran. He was lodged in the house of an old woman of the island Mahal [Male]. One day he visited his hostess and found that she had assembled her relatives, and that the women were weeping as at a funeral. He questioned them upon the subject of their affliction, but they could not make him understand the cause, until an interpreter, who chanced to come in, informed him that the lot had fallen upon the old woman, and that she had an only daughter, who was now about to be slain by the evil Jinni. Abú'l-barakát said to the woman: 'I will go to-night in thy daughter's stead.' At that time he was entirely beardless. So, on the night following, after he had completed his ablutions, he was conducted to the idol temple. On arrival there he set himself to recite the Koran. Presently, through the window, beholding the demon to approach, he continued his recitation. The Jinni, as soon as he came within hearing of the Koran, plunged into the sea and disappeared; and so it was that, when the dawn was come, the Maghrabin was still occupied in reciting the Koran. When the old woman, her relatives, and the people of the island, according to their custom, came to take away the girl and burn the corpse, they found the stranger reciting the Koran. They conducted him to their King, by name Shanúrdza, whom they informed of this adventure. The King was astonished; and the Maghrabin both proposed to him to embrace the true faith, and inspired him with a desire for it. Then said Shanúrdza to him: 'Remain with us until next month, and if you do again as you have now done and escape the evil Jinni, I will be converted'. Wherefore the stranger remained with the idolaters, and God disposed the heart of the King to receive the true faith. He became Musalmán before the end of the month, as well as his wives, children, and courtiers. At the beginning of the following month the Maghrabin was conducted again to the idol temple; but the Jinni came not, and the Berber recited the Koran till the morning, when the Sultan and his subjects arrived and found him so employed. Then they broke the idols, and razed the temple to the ground. The people of the island embraced Islam, and sent messengers to the other islands, whose inhabitants were also converted.

*Ibn Battuta, translated by Albert Gray, 1888*

Ibn Battuta (1304-1368), the greatest Muslim traveller of the Middle Ages, was born in Tangier. He devoted almost 30 years to journeys as far as Kilwa on the East African coast; into the basin of the Volga; to Sumatra and China; and across northwest Africa to the basin of the Niger and back to Morocco.

occasion Malabari troops certainly were used, together with Portuguese soldiers they met on the short voyage from southern India to the Maldives. This alliance proved costly to the Sultan, as the Portuguese claimed an annual tribute payable to their viceroy in Goa, which later led them to establish a presence in Malé by force in 1517, in effect annexing the country. This first European foray was cut short by troops lent by the ruler of Cochin.

Freedom was short-lived, however, as a few years later another ruler, Sultan Hassan IX, was deposed after showing too little respect for Islam. Fleeing to Cochin, he was met by the Jesuit missionary, St Francis Xavier who baptized him a Christian and renamed him Don Emanuel. He stayed in Cochin for two years before moving up the coast to Goa where he married a Portuguese noblewoman. Aided by the troublesome Portuguese, former Sultan Hassan-Emanuel led two expeditions to regain control over the Maldives: both were unsuccessful.

In fact, the Portuguese had ideas of their own for the Maldives and in 1558 sent an expedition under a Captain Andreas Andre. According to Maldivian legend, this commander was born in the Maldives, his mother being the wife of a ship's captain who was also commander of the forces raised against Kulu Umbushumu who in turn destroyed the Portuguese fleet and killed everyone on board except this woman, Captain Andre's mother. Taking her to his island, he later married her; her child grew up to be known as Andiri Andirin.

As a young man he escaped to Goa, only to return years later as commander of the Portuguese forces. He annihilated the Maldivians under Sultan Ali VI, who died in the heat of battle, while fortifying himself from a coconut full of toddy.

# The Portuguese

For the next 17 years, the Portuguese under Andreas Andre were the rulers of the Maldives, in the name of King Hassan-Emanuel. Local historians brood over this period as the darkest hour of their nation's history, a time when men were treated as slaves, women were violated at whim, deputies extended a reign of terror to the outer atolls, and the Europeans generally tried to force everyone to become Christian. François Pyrard de Laval notes thoughtfully, however, that people told him only a few decades later that trade had never been as good as when the Portuguese were in charge.

Redemption for the Maldives came in the form of Mohamed Thakurufaanu, born on the distant island of Utheemu, and prophetically on the very same day as Andreas Andre. He and his two brothers, one of whom was beheaded by the Portuguese, built a fast boat in which they embarked upon a form of guerilla warfare—hit-and-run tactics that weakened the Portuguese without challenging them seriously (though one local historian has suggested their feats were 'sometimes bordering on the supernatural').

Malé, they decided, was too hard for them to take on single-handed, so they sought assistance from the Rajah of Cannanore. Thakurufaanu returned in 1573 on the night a Portuguese ultimatum to the Maldivian elders expired. This obliged them to convert to Christianity or be put to the sword. Placing his Malabari troops in positions around the town, he managed to infiltrate a party into the Portuguese encampment and shoot Andre from behind a coconut tree—a nice Maldivian touch that makes the legend seem quite real, especially as, miraculously, the tree also deflected the bullet that Andre fired back. A fierce battle ensued in which the Portuguese were all killed, eventually leaving Thakurufaanu in charge as Sultan Ghazi Muhammad Thakurufan al-Auzam.

The Portuguese tried on several further occasions to retake the Maldives in order to install a puppet regime with the grandchildren of King Hassan-Emanuel. These all failed, after which the Portuguese left the Maldives in peace. Thakurufaanu ruled with his brother, eventually dying in 1585. He is credited with having minted the first local coins, forming a trained standing army, and improving religious observance and trade.

Thakurufaanu's son, Sultan Kalaafannu, fared less fortunately and was killed by a bunch of marauding Malabari pirates who caught him on the high seas fleeing south and then proceeded to plunder Malé and destroy the royal palace. An official expedition was mounted in the mid-seventeenth century by the Rajah of Cannanore when Sultan Iskander I withheld payment of the tribute that had been paid for over a century and a half since the time of Sultan Kulu Muhammad. After a brief struggle the position was reversed, with the Maldivian sultan persuading the inhabitants of Minicoy, a small group of islands just north of the Maldives and under the Rajah's rule, to pay him tribute instead.

## Pyrard's Adventures

François Pyrard de Laval was a Frenchman who sailed in 1601 from St Malo en route for the East Indies. Fourteen months after leaving France his ship, the *Corbin*, was shipwrecked on a Maldivian reef while the captain was sick and the watch drunk or asleep. Some of the crew escaped only to be flung into the Portuguese galleys, but Pyrard himself was held captive in Malé for five years, earning the trust of the sultan

*The carved wooden ceiling of the Friday Mosque, Malé*

by his alacrity in learning the language. Eventually he was rescued by a fleet from Chittagong, which arrived to try to salvage the *Corbin's* cannons.

Pyrard then began his long journey home, which serendipitously took him to Brazil before finally landing in Spain in 1611, a decade after he left Europe. His account, the first full-length one of the Maldives and the Malabar coast of India, made him famous. It has only been matched by an account by two British naval officers, Christopher and Powell, who visited the islands in the 1830s.

The story he unfolds is of an autocratic sultan to whom everything shipwrecked on the many reefs belonged, and for whose subjects it was treason to leave the country without permission. However, Pyrard became something of a celebrity at court, the sultan's wives asking him many questions about the French court and being amazed that the French king only had one wife. He found the people 'cunning in trade and in social life'. The women grew their hair long, well oiled, and stuffed with false hair culled from the menfolk of the Malabars. Hirsute men were despised; children of both sexes had their's shorn every week until the age of nine, and old men shaved their torsos into strange patterns as though they were wearing a slashed doublet. Pyrard's main complaint was that they used blunt razors that always drew blood, though everyone pretended—with Maldivian machismo—that it didn't hurt at all.

He learned Dhivehi, and some Arabic which he observed is learned 'by them as Latin is with us'. He recorded the love rituals of gifts of betel and sonnets between youngsters, and the rule that a man with three wives must sleep with all three equally regularly. 'It is but an ill-considered law for these countries where three husbands would not suffice for one wife, so lewd are the women,' he observed caustically. An anthropologist with an eye for fashion, Pyrard noted the silk petticoats and the robes of taffeta or fine cotton, and the gold bracelets that could only be worn with the permission of the sultana. He noted also the women's winsome figures, that they were always well turned out, and the 'country notion of beauty' of painting their toe and fingernails red.

Pyrard was impressed by the Maldivians' consistent hospitality among themselves and their fastidiousness in preparing food and eating, and their habit of discarding broken crockery, which they used instead of gold and silver (as this was forbidden, even for the sultan). He was similarly horrified by their rampant superstition and by 'their indulgence of women, lascivious and intemperate'. He wrote that 'adultery, incest and sodomy are common, notwithstanding the severity of the law and penalties. . . the women are strangely wanton, and the men no better. . . their chief desire is to find, if they can, some recipe wherewithal to satisfy their wives. . . and I believe they would give all their substance for such a thing. They have often asked me if I knew of any such means, even the highest nobles, and so often, that I was quite sick of the subject.' He added that they were addicted to opium and that common talk of sex was shunned. Politely, he forbears to describe this as straightforward hypocrisy.

He observed summary judgments in the courts and lashings, along with the orchards and gardens of the king's palace, the raised floors to escape the ants and the beds suspended from the ceiling so as to rock the wealthy to sleep. Apparently the sultana and her retinue lived behind five hangings of cloth in an apartment without natural light.

All was peaceful in the Maldives until 1752 when the younger brother of Iskander I, Sultan Muhammad Imaduddin III, was deposed by invading Malabaris under Ali Rajah for about four months. Then another hero, Hassan Manikfan, duped the Malabaris into retiring to bed early one night and massacred the lot of them. When the rajah sent another force to retake Malé, Hassan ran up the Malabari flag at the port entrance and sent out a welcoming party disguised as Malabaris, conning the fleet into entering the harbour unawares only to be destroyed by cannon fire. A third invasion was foiled after Hassan enlisted the help of the French at Pondicherry under Captain Le Termellier, and the Dutch who helped destroy the Malabari fleet at sea. Hassan in time became Sultan Al Ghazi Hassan Izzaddin.

# The British

Relative freedom lasted until 1887 when Sultan Muhammad Muenuddin signed an agreement with the British governor of Ceylon turning the Maldives into a British protectorate on payment of an annual tribute. This arrangement left the sultans ruling as autocrats until 1932 when a new constitution was adopted and a republic briefly declared. However, royal power returned soon afterwards. Following the independence of India and Shri Lanka after the Second World War, the British dropped the requirement for tribute, and finally a republic was declared in 1953. The first president, Amin Didi, was, however, overthrown after a coup and died a prisoner on Vihamanafushi, now the resort island of Kurumba. Once again the Maldives reverted to a sultanate.

The British, however, were interested in using the strategic southern atolls and established an RAF base on Gan in 1957, an unpopular decision in Malé which led to the resignation of the prime minister. This coincided with a period of unrest in the three southernmost atolls which felt the central authorities in far-off Malé were making life unduly harsh for them, especially by forcing them to call in at Malé before sailing off to trade with India and Shri Lanka. A rebel government in the south declared itself independent as the United Suvadive Atolls under one Abdulla Afeef; it managed to hold out against government forces without guns for around four years, but in the end was spirited away to exile in the Seychelles.

The British continued leasing the airfield facilities on Gan until 1976, when the Labour government decided it was too expensive to maintain. The Russians then said they wanted to use Gan—450 miles north of the strategic US naval and air base on Diego Garcia—for the Soviet fishing fleet. They offered the Maldivians a small rent, but President Nasir upped the price and asked for $1 million. According to a report in the *Asian Wall Street Journal*, a Soviet diplomat complained angrily to a Western colleague that 'you could buy the whole country for $1 million'. And so the deal fell through. Maldivians remember things differently, viewing the rent as bait to allow the Russians to avoid Maldivian customs and immigration checks, which would have effectively barred Maldivians from Gan altogether.

# Independence

The Maldives were granted full independence on 26 July 1965. The reigning sultan, the 94th, Muhammad Fareed I, lasted another three years before a republic was declared after a referendum, and the hero of the anti-British protests, Ibrahim Nasir, became the first president. He held office until his resignation in 1978, followed by his sudden departure and self-imposed retirement in Singapore. He was later sentenced to 25 years' banishment in absentia for fermenting rebellion and plotting a coup.

President Maumoon Abdul Gayoom, the current incumbent, has been re-elected twice, the last occasion being in 1988 with more than 96 per cent of the vote, an achievement unmatched outside of the former Soviet satellite countries of eastern Europe. He was the target of a second coup attempt in November 1988, when a tropical fish exporter, Abdulla Luthufi, tried to seize power using mercenaries from one of the Tamil independence factions in neighbouring Shri Lanka. The mercenaries proved very incompetent, and the insurrection was finally put down by Rajiv Gandhi's troops during one of the Indian leader's expansionary phases. Dozens of people were sentenced to death and later banished after public trials in Malé a year later.

The Maldives' security force has since been sufficiently strengthened to prevent any such further attempt on the sovereignty of the country, and the government called for an international force to help protect vulnerable states from aggression, a move supported by the UN.

Since achieving independence in 1965, the Maldives has charted an independent course for itself as a member of the British Commonwealth, a non-aligned state within the United Nations, and a loyal Muslim nation. It ranks as the 117th state in the United Nations and is its smallest member.

## Changing Times

Malé enjoyed something of a boom in the 1970s when hundreds of Indian traders made regular visits to take advantage of the duty-free regulations, a form of commuter smuggling that the Indians cracked down on after a few years. The dried fish industry boomed for a while but collapsed just as the tourist industry was getting off the ground in 1972. Government policy now is to push the resorts up-market, to get the 'value-added' tourist. Backpackers are strictly discouraged. Under President Nasir, islands could be sold outright, but this policy was changed in the 1980s and the 'lost' islands nationalized. Resorts are now leased by the government, instead of being sold.

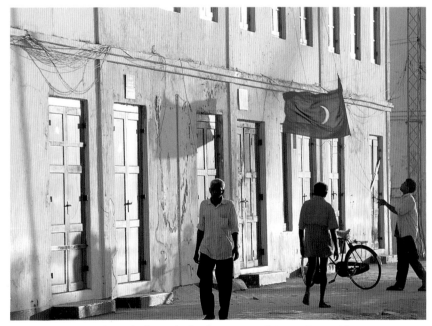

*Lowering the flag as the day draws to an end, Marine Drive, Malé*

Much recent construction work, such as the airport runway extension, has been funded by loans from friendly Arab nations like Saudi Arabia. Malé's breakwater was rebuilt in 1987 partly with Japanese money, and partly with a loan from the Asian Development Bank, which is basically Japanese-funded.

Many people feel the Maldives is changing rapidly. The days when massive sail-driven *buggalows* took three days to sail to Shri Lanka are now a distant memory. Traditions of warmth and hospitality—especially the practice of *mutaa*, or short-term marriage of convenience—have often been abused by visitors in the past. So nowadays, for example, a foreigner who wishes to marry a Maldivian has to change his religion and name, become a Muslim, and register these facts on his passport.

Life in the Maldives has certainly changed, but compared with the recent past much of the change has been distinctly positive. In 1965 there were no social welfare programmes in the Maldives. There was a high rate of infant mortality and communicable diseases were prevalent. Yet by 1977, life expectancy had been raised from 46 to 62 years, and infant mortality cut by a third. While English had been banned by the sultans until as recently as 50 years ago, an English language school was established in Malé in 1961.

# Culture

Maldivian myths and folklore are focused on the sea, reflecting the local lifestyle which revolves around the changing seasons and the size of the fishing catch—as befits a tiny, remote island nation. This natural rhythm is threatened, however, as with other isolated cultures, by the increase of international tourism, the importation of western goods, and the evidence of growing wealth accumulated by some islanders. Many young Maldivians dream of making it big in Malé rather than staying in a small fishing village in a far-flung atoll. Looked at another way, today's international tourists are just the latest in a long history of visitors which started with the earliest traders two millenia or more ago. These early traders, whose boats made use of favourable winds to round the tip of the Indian subcontinent to ply between the East Indies and Africa, are long gone, but their influence and presence can still be felt.

Maldivians, or the *Divi* as they were known to ancient Roman and Arabic chroniclers, are a Dravidian people, a mix of Indian, Sinhalese, and Tamil cultures with even earlier roots reaching back to East Africa and Arabia. Modern historians believe the strongest affinities are with the Sinhalese of Shri Lanka, whose ancestors spoke an Indo-Aryan language and originally sailed south from the northwest Indian coast. The earliest inhabitants of Shri Lanka, however, were Tamil speakers, and according to the explorer Thor Heyerdahl, many words in the Maldivian language, especially those to express kinship and the finer points of ocean navigation, are obviously Tamil in origin. The word *dhoni* for example, comes from Tamil.

It is believed that the very first settlers of the Maldives—mostly lost fishermen, shipwrecked sailors, and their descendants from South India—were Hindu. But the Aryans who colonized the islands later, brought their own religion and a language called *ellu*, a Sanskrit-based language which is close to a very pure form of the Sinhalese spoken in Shri Lanka today.

## Dhivehi Script and Language

The Maldives' official language is called Dhivehi, which also gives its name to the country, *Dhivehi raajje* (Dhivehi speakers), and the people *Dhivehin* (islanders). Although this is derived from the *ellu* tongue, it can be considered a corruption of Sanskrit, the language that spread out from the Indus Valley region after the year 1,500 BC as the great Indo-Aryan civilization collapsed, extending across most of the subcontinent and the Near East. Present-day Dhivehi has acquired words from other sources, including Malayalam, Arabic and Tamil.

The earliest Maldivian script was known as *evayla* and was written left to right in the same manner as the roman script. This was superceded by another called *dhives akuru*, which was also written from left to right, and which was itself replaced four centuries ago by the script in current use, called *thaana akuru*, which has more Arabic-style characters and has changed to right to left to accommodate them.

Although Arabic letters had been familiar since the introduction of the Koran 800 years ago, the Maldivians have continued using their own *thaana* script. They were obviously a literate nation even before the Arabs came and examples of their earliest script are preserved in several ancient copper books known as *loamaafaanu*, the earliest of which dates back to 1195. The modern *thaana* script resembles a series of tiger paw prints, or a snake wriggling across the sand, fat squiggles which do not appear as refined or elegant as the scimitar-thin swirls and loops of classical Arabic. Like other language forms, including Chinese, there's no exact correlation between *thaana* and our roman script so modern spellings of the same word or name can vary enormously; thus *Dhivehi* and *Divehi* are both in common usage.

A borrower from many tongues, as befits its trading crossroads history, the Maldives is proud that, despite its small size, Dhivehi has contributed one word—atoll—into the everyday usage of the English language.

# Dhoni Construction

The basic design of the traditional Maldivian seagoing vessel has changed little during recorded times. Timber from the coconut palm is still used, though these days some imported wood is also used to strengthen the structure of the hull. These resilient little craft are built by master carpenters using very few tools and no plans. Their skills are passed down from generation to generation within the same families in a genuine, living, oral tradition.

The boats are usually built inside coconut-thatched huts set at the water's edge. On some outer islands boat building supports the economy of the entire community. Boat carpenters are known as *kissaru vadin*, literally 'curved carpenters', and they command not only a high wage but a lot of respect within the community. Completing a *dhoni* can take two months as one of these craftsmen builds a 12-metre (40-foot) boat using only an axe, an adze to dress the wood, a drill made of a wooden hammer and an iron bit, a chisel, a mallet and a hammer.

The hull of the *dhoni* is called the *fashan*, and is made from planks of hardwood taken from the base of the tree and fitted together with wooden nails so that the

# Creatures of the Deep

They have an admirable quantitie of great Fish, as Bonitos, Albachores, guilt-heads and others which are very like one another, and of the same taste, and have no more skales then the Mackrell. They take them in the deepe Sea, on this fashion, with a line of a fathom and a halfe of great round Cotton thred made fast to a great Cane. Their hooke, is not so much bowed as ours, but more stretched out, & is pointed in the end like a Pin, without having any other beard or tonge. They fasten not on their Bait, but the day before provide a quantitie of small Fish, as great as our little Bleaks, or Roches, which they find in great number on the Bankes and Sands, and keep them alive inclosed in little pursnets (made of the Thred of Cocos) with little Mashes, and let them hang in the Sea at the Sterne of their Barkes. When they come into the deepe Sea, they sow about their little Fishes, and let their Line hang downe. The great Fish seeing the little Fish, which is not frequent in the deepe Sea, runne together in great shoales, and by the same meanes they fasten them to their hookes, which they white and trim over; so that being a ravenous and foolish Fish, it takes the whited Hook, thinking it is a white little Fish. They doe nothing but lift their Line into their Boat, and the Fish falls off presently (being not strongly fastened) and then they put it into the Sea againe; thus they take a strange quantitie, so that in three or foure houres their Boates are in a manner full; and that which is remarkable, they go alwayes with full sayle. The Fish which they take thus they generally cal in their language Cobolly Masse, that is to say, the Blacke Fish, for they are all blacke.

They have another sort of fishing on their bankes, when the Moone is in the change, and when it is at the full, three daies eacha time. This they doe on Rafts made of the Wood, called Camdou. They have great Lines of fiftie or sixtie fathome pitched over. In the end they hang hookes wheron they fasten the baite as we doe, and thus take great quantitie of fish, one kinde very delicious, which they call the King of the Sea. They have all sorts of Nets and Toiles made of Cotton twine, Weeles and other Instruments of fishing. Neere the Sea shoare, and where it is shallow, they passe their time, and take delight in fishing for small fish, like Pilchards with casting Nets. Twice in the Yueere at the Equinoctials, they make a generall fishing, a great number of persons assemble together in certaine indraughts of the Sea. The Sea at that time ariseth higher then all the times of the Yeere, and passeth the limits of other Tides, the Ebbe after the same proportion recoiles and retires, discovering these Rockes and Shoalds, which at other times appeare not. In these places while the Sea is going out, they observe some fit corner, and set about it great stones, one upon another to a great height, so that it resembles a round Wall or Raveling. This inclosure hath forties paces in circuit or compasse: but the entrance is but two or three paces large. They gather together thritie or fortie men, and every one carrieth fiftie or sixie fathome of great coard of Cocos, where from fathome to fathome they tie a piece of the Barke of dried Cocos, to make it float on the water, as we use Corke: after, they tye them together, and stretch them out in a round upon the flats. It is strange, that all the fish which is within the coard, finding themselves taken, although there bee no other Nets nor Instruments, but the Coard which swimmeth on the water, but the fish fearing the Line and shadow of the Line; so that they dare not passe under to escape, but flye from the Line, thinking that it hath a Net underneath: The men goe all driving them to the inclsure of stone, drawing up the coard by little and little some in Boates, and some in the water (for upon these flats the Sea is shallow, and not above necke high for the most part lesse) so moderately drawing up the Line, the fish flye from it, and are locked up in the inclosure, so that in the end yhᵉ Line being all drawne up, all the fishes enter in: and they speedily stop the entry with Faggots of boughes and leaves of Cocos, bound end to end, twentie or thirtie fathome, and compacted together about the greatnesse of a man, and so when the Sea is out, the fish remaine taken on the dry Land. They often take thus of all sorts ten and twelve thousand or more. This fishing they make but once in sixe monethes, upon every flat, and everytime continues five daies, and they change daily their divisions, and returne not often into the same place to fish in this manner, except at another Equinoctiall.

François Pyrard de Laval
Hakluytus Posthumus or Purchas His Pilgrimes, 1905

entire boat fits together like an interlocking jigsaw. This structure is secured by pounding brass or copper nails into the wooden slats. Fish oil is then smoothed over the hulls of the *masdhoni* fishing boats, partly to aid its passage through the water and in the belief that it will ensure a good catch.

## The Family

A well-defined division of labour exists within the Maldivian family, another age-old pattern that has yet to be widely disrupted by the onrush of progress. All outdoor work, the major part of which consists of fishing, is carried out by the men. The traditional function of women, aside from bearing children and doing the household chores, is to help process the fish and the breadfruit crop, to weave copra fibre and screw pine leaves into cloth and mats, and to collect cowrie shells from the beach.

Maldivian women are, however, accorded more freedom than in many other traditional Islamic societies. The practice of purdah was never wholly accepted, though veils were commonly used at different times in the past. The Maldivian national dress for women includes a snippet-like veil that continues to be worn to this day. Women are not expected to bring a dowry with them at marriage, neither are men required to pay more than a nominal bride price over and above the expenses of the wedding. Marriage does not diminish a woman's social status unduly, and as long as she adheres to Islamic codes no other rigid curbs are imposed, though individual sultans and *qazis* have held different views on the benefits of female emancipation or women's full participation in society.

In a country where the law is heavily biased in favour of men, women may appear to be at a disadvantage, especially in male-dominated courts. Marriage is usually conducted in the groom's house. Once he has the agreement of the girl, he informs the local Islamic judge, the *qazi*, who confirms her acquiescence. The wedding itself is a minor affair, which the bride does not usually even attend, with just two witnesses to confirm the action of the *qazi*. The act of divorce, *vari*, like that of marriage, is carried out in accordance with religious law, the *sharia*. Thus a woman cannot terminate her marriage without her husband's consent, though a man can dump his wife merely by uttering the words *kaley thiya inee vari koffa*, or 'I divorce you', three times and then settling on her a reasonable amount of maintenance money. However, if a married man dies, his spouse is entitled to the proceeds of his estate.

Polygamy, another ancient practice, still exists, though is less common these days. The Islamic variation forbids any man more than three wives at any one time;

and he must prove he is able to support all of them. Sultans traditionally always had three wives, but the institution of a harem, as occurred regularly in India, has never existed in the Maldives. The seventeenth-century French explorer, François Pyrard de Laval, relates an eyewitness account of a man who married and divorced 80 or 100 times during his lifetime. A contemporary Maldivian merchant, for instance, may still have two or three wives and live within his extended family, while a struggling fisherman on an outer island is probably thankful to have just one to support.

# Fishing

Fishing is by a long chalk the most ubiquitous, and economically and socially the most important activity in the Maldives, a community affair throughout the atolls, particularly in the outer islands. The owner of a boat, the *masdhoni*, receives around 20-35 per cent of the catch plus one fish per member of the crew in payment for prayers said for them while at sea, a practice that varies from island to island. The remainder is shared among the crew members, with the chief fisherman (*keolu*) getting the lion's share, followed by the chief bait fisherman, the *en keolu*.

The day starts very early as the bait fish have to be caught well before sunrise in the shallows of the lagoon. They are kept in a special compartment on board the *dhoni* so it looks to a foreign eye as if the boat is slowly flooding. Once at sea, the crew look out for circling flocks of birds which will show them where to find the tuna. They then throw the live bait overboard and beat the water from the stern end of the boat to induce the tuna into a feeding frenzy. The fishermen swiftly and deftly set about hooking a big fish, landing it, then hooking another. Each man can catch up to 100 fish in an hour, literally picking them out of the water. The catch is normally sold on the beach. Fine tuna is transported to Japan to be made into sashimi. Back on shore the village awaits the boats' return with anticipation. Even suppliers on the island providing sails and hooks will be paid in kind rather than cash.

# Entertainment and Games

In the age before television, diversions and amusements were generated from within society as an expression of their togetherness, usually through movement or music. With the strictures of Islam firmly observed in the Maldives, it is usually only the men who get to dance, such behaviour being considered most unseemly for girls who

*Children of Thoddu*

have passed puberty ('hanging loose' is definitely something that only men should do). Dances are usually performed to celebrate special occasions and are ritualized around specific ceremonies and rites of passage like male circumcision. Visitors will probably be shown a local 'cultural performance' at their resort, performed either by a travelling troupe of professional dancers or more likely by the resort's kitchen staff after hours.

The best known traditional Maldivian dance is *bodu beru*, thought to have been brought to the Maldives by African settlers as long ago as the 12th century. The musical instruments are usually a trio of coconut-wood drums lashed tautly with the hide of a stingray, a small bell, and an *onugadu*, a piece of bamboo in which notches have been cut to produce an eerie, gamelan-like sound. The band is accompanied by about 15 *lungi*-clad male dancers who start gyrating in a very slow, swaying rhythm, throwing their arms about and gradually becoming progressively wilder and more frantic as they continue late into the night. One type of *bodu*, called the *tara*, was recently banned because frenzied dancers climaxed the performance by repeatedly bashing their heads with spiked clubs until their blood ran. An Indian-style *bandiyya jehun* is a gentler harvest or fertility dance, performed by very young women who beat metallic water pots in time to an accompanying song. *Gaa odi lava* is a dance traditionally performed before the sultan as an expression of gratitude for his benevolence. The dancers move around a box that in the old days held the sultan's gift of money. As with most Maldivian dances, it starts slowly but the tempo increases as it progresses.

The songs accompanying these dances are sung in a mixture of Arabic and Dhivehi, while some words apparently derive from languages from central Africa. The oldest form of folk music is known as *thaara*, said to have been introduced by the Persians and the Arabs in the 17th century. Its chanted lyrics are uttered in Arabic and accompanied by a multi-drum rhythm section of great virtuosity. *Raivaru* is an old type of poetry few can understand today, intoned in a dragging, repetitive tune often accompanied by a slow dance. The sentiments expressed are very often in code language and can be difficult even for Maldivians to decipher.

Maldivians are not much into games. One you might see is known as *bai bala*, a wrestling sport in which a single player enters a ring and attempts to touch members of the opposite team. If he can escape without being helped out of the ring then all those whom he has touched are eliminated. *Mandi* is a traditional sport in which a small stick is propelled by players with slightly longer sticks. Opponents are required to catch it without letting it drop to the ground, a bit like a stick version of the 'hakky-sack' game played in Vietnam and certain English schools with a small hide-covered ball. A popular children's game is *gandu filla*. Here a player has to be identi-fied by the opposite team while the other members of his team usually remain hidden, a bit like hide-and-seek with a detective element tagged on. A variation of chess exists but with slightly modified rules. The traditional Arabic game of *carrom*, a bit like cueless billards, is also played, plus a board game called *ovvalu* which uses money cowries placed in little dips in the board, a good teaching aid to get children to count.

If you develop a taste for Maldivian music, or if you want to purchase a cassette as a curiosity to give to your friends, you can find tapes of famous Maldivian love songs and *bodu beri* music in several music stores in Malé. The John Lennon of the Maldives is called Hassan Fulu. But on the whole, popular culture doesn't reach much beyond imported music and the ubiquitous Hindi movies from Bombay. Only one 35mm feature film has been made locally in the entire history of the country, a Maldivian-Egyptian co-production called 'Youssef and Zeinab' filmed in 1986. The plot centres, not surprisingly, on an Egyptian man visiting the Maldives to teach English, who falls in love with a local Maldivian girl. There are no plans for a sequel.

# Crafts

Indigenous crafts are thin on the ground. The best *kunaar*, mats made from leaves of the screw pine, are said to be dyed, woven, and hand-printed on Gaddu in Gaafu-Dhaalu Atoll. The finest lacquerwork is reputed to originate from Thulhaadhoo in Baa Atoll. Lengths of traditional *feyli* cloth are also woven in Baa. Carved wooden models of *dhonis* often come from islands in North Maalhosmadulu Atoll. Modern gold jewellery is made in Ribudhu, silver in Hulhudheli, both of them islands in South Nilandhe Atoll. Black coral and mother-of-pearl may likely come from Lhaviyani Atoll. Fish bones decorated with black coral or mother-of-pearl are also made by local artisans, though the red coral made in Dhaal Atoll is imported from China. (Note. Avoid buying black coral products as it is endangered world-wide, and cannot be legally imported into many countries.)

# Architecture

On the outer islands, untouched by developments in Malé, whose modern houses have little charm, you can still see the unique style of traditional Maldivian architecture which makes ingenious use of natural fibres and materials. Coral serves as both bricks and mortar; burned slowly in deep pits, it yields a powerful lime cement. Houses are constructed almost entirely of coral slates and *cadjan* (coconut leaf-thatched roofs), and enclosed by a coral wall around a garden, usually above its own water well. These walls are about head height to ensure some privacy since the enclosure serves as a traditional Maldivian open-air bathroom. Some tourist resorts have adopted this design in their huts; few experiences can be more pleasant than lying in an open-air bath raised above the coral sand, surrounded by fragrant frangipani and screw pine bushes yet privately open to the sky. Powdered coral sand is used to surface the floors and the surrounding garden area, and most households have their own well sunk to a depth of about two metres (six feet) to tap the rain-filled—and these days invariably brackish—water-table under most islands. Water is drawn from this *gifili* with the aid of a long wooden pole armed at its end with a large ladle called a *dhaani*.

One of the pleasing aspects of the Maldives is that everything is kept so spotlessly clean. Coral paths are brushed each day and many everyday objects are made out of natural, rather than man-made, materials. Coconut husks are turned into coir for matting; screw pine husks are woven and hand-printed into aesthetic decorations called *thudu kunaa*, while the leaves are turned into baskets. Special *cadjan* mats are made from large coconut leaves woven together with coir rope to form roof-thatching material. Wood is very scarce in the Maldives so houses are quite devoid of it. Indeed it is so precious that there is a special market in Malé for imported fire wood.

Rooms are often small, but the furnishings are neat and simple. A flat bench serves as a rudimentary bed at night and a place to sit during the day. Tucked under the bed is usually a heavy wooden chest where the family's worldly goods and treasures are stored. The lack of furniture is really unimportant as families spend most of their time outside on the veranda, the social focus of the home, where they can sit under the shade of a leafy breadfruit tree as protection against the relentless sun. It is usual to find an *undoali* strung up, a large wooden swing in which to idle away the hours. There are also hammock-style chairs known as *joali* made from wood and coir rope. Domestic craftsmen are known as *ted ui vadin*, and generally every inhabited island has one who turns out chests, tables, and swings.

# Modern life

Many young Maldivians are eager to taste the outside world, though this desire for liberty is not encouraged by the government which operates what amounts to a work in return for study scheme, so that every Maldivian going overseas to study has to dedicate extra years on his return to his already statutory period of government service—a move that tends to dampen the brightest and focus restless minds

## WITCH DOCTORS

Superstition still rules the lives of many Maldive islanders. Evil spirits like the *jinni*, and the amorphous *dhevi*, are thought to come from the sea, land and sky. Their machinations can account for everything that cannot be explained by either religion or education.

Historians say these beliefs arose long before the arrival of Islam in the Maldives, at a time when its people felt themselves simultaneously at one and at the mercy of the primordial natural forces surrounding them in their island world. To please and appease the forces of nature, these spirits had to be worshipped. According to an ancient Maldivian myth, one evil spirit called the *Rannamaari* was a particularly truculent *jinni* which several centuries ago required the regular sacrifice of virgins. Adherents catalogue more than 50 categories of spirit which require a variety of incarnations. One spirit resembles a horse with a light coming from its forehead, another an old woman, a third a shadow that can appear in the shape of a human being or a grey monkey, or with an elephant's trunk, as a tortoise, or covered in sparks of fire, or as a seven-headed woman. Some spirits induce epilepsy, madness, or death. Beneficent ones can repair rotten teeth, but most prefer to suck blood from human veins, make *dhonis* run aground, or sexually molest women.

The only weapon to combat the evil *jinnis* are the *fanditha* —the name literally means 'to cast out'—which are the spells and lotions concocted by the local *hakeem* or witchdoctor, a village man who acts as a combination of exorcist, conjurer, herbalist, and astrologer. He becomes qualified to practise the art of *fanditha* only after passing an arcane examination, mysterious to all non-initiates. The *hakeem* is often called upon when

inwards. Nevertheless, the outside world is spreading its tentacles farther and farther, year by year, despite the careful segregation of tourists from as many of the native population as possible. In the past, the Maldives was a mecca in its own right for Indians seeking cheap electronic goods to take back to their homeland. Today, most Indians prefer to go to Singapore to pick up their cheap electronic goods to smuggle past the abnormally alert customs officials back home. Malé's shops instead display items coveted by the growing Maldivian middle class, including many objects whose usefulness is of dubious taste.

illness strikes, if a woman fails to conceive, or if the fishing catch is consistently poor. He might cast a curing spell by writing phrases from the Koran on strips of paper, sticking or tying them to the patient while reciting the sayings out loud. Another method is to write them in ink on a plate that is then filled with water and given to the patient to drink. Traditional Maldivian medicine, known as *divei bais*, is prepared by the *hakeem* from local and imported herbs and is remarkably similar to the traditional herbal medicines of the Orient.

Other concoctions include *isitri*, a love potion used by unrequited lovers to enhance their powers of attraction (its antidote, *varitoli* is used to break up marriages). Considering the frequency of divorce in the Maldives this does not appear to be used very often, but according to a *hakeem* I spoke to, the consequences of an *istiri* or *varitoli* that backfires can be disastrous. Clairvoyance is known as *faalu* and is used both to predict the future and locate missing objects, or even to obtain the description of a person suspected of committing an offence.

*Fanditha* charms are used primarily to heal or to encourage the environment to behave more favourably, like providing better fishing catches. However, the practice of *sihuru*, Maldivian sorcery and black magic, can land an advocate in very deep trouble and even a period of banishment from society to a remote island. Other forms of good magic exist, such as *nadhuru*, a sacred vow pledged to perform a good deed if and when the desired preconditions are fulfilled. This might involve anything from a simple to an elaborate sacrifice, or the giving of alms. When a child becomes sick, bananas or *nadhuru folhi*, a wafer-thin pancake equal to the weight of the child, are sometimes distributed.

# Crime and Punishment

The Maldives follows a moderate version of the Islamic legal code, the *sharia*, which does not compel women to wear the *chador*, stone adulterers, or chop off the hands of thieves. It has, however, refined its own form of an ancient punishment: banishment to a remote island, usually for eight months, or sometimes for one or two years. This cuts off the prisoners from all family ties. While at first encountering a hostile reaction from local inhabitants and being treated as pariahs, they are later often accepted in their cuckoo community, a curiously effective form of social rehabilitation. The system was introduced by the Maldivian royal family as means of controlling troublesome rivals. African slaves, thought to have been brought back from the *Hajj* pilgrimage to Mecca, were often very rebellious and found themselves consigned to Felidhu in Ari Atoll.

Banishment is meted out today for a range of offences, mainly religious ones. These include the secret tippling of alcohol, premarital sex, stealing, and wilful breaking of the Ramadan fast. Since the community is so small there is hardly any privacy and infractions are hard to hide and easily unmasked. Lashings are also given to lesser offenders by those described to me by the chief judge in Malé as 'certain trained people'. These chastisements take place in the court room with an instrument that looks like a long cook's ladle topped by an oblong handle which delivers a hearty thwack without drawing blood. By constitution it is the president who can commute, lessen or parden a sentence passed. Otherwise it is up to a clutch of *qazis*, the judges that sit in the jury-free Islamic court. They obviously have a lot to do despite the Maldivians' generally placid nature and easy-going life-style. Every inhabited island has a court, and Malé has eight! Despite this, the coun-

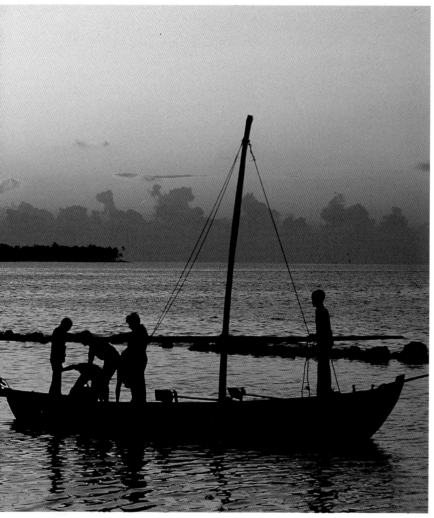

*Preparing to set out for a day's work*

try doesn't even have a prison to hold its criminal offenders, though one island is in effect a high-security prison where the leaders of the 1988 coup attempt are serving out their life banishment.

In recent times, an increasing number of citizens have been banished for embezzlement and fraud, a knock-on effect of the influx of new wealth as Maldivians aspire to become richer. Malé is hardly New York though; there hasn't been a case of murder, other than one committed by a foreigner, since 1953. And the Attorney General thinks that crime can be all but eradicated by promoting volleyball, cricket and other sports, and encouraging people to eat more fish.

The etiquette of conviction is as bizarre as the punishments that the guilty receive. Suspects have to be personally accused in a courtroom confrontation, something completely alien to most western countries. Unmarried lovers or adulterers have to be confronted by no less than four witnesses, which would seem to leave the door wide open to promiscuity (or tightly bolted, depending on your point of view). It is considered very bad form to accuse someone with only circumstantial evidence to back up the claim.

The catalogue of potential crimes makes interesting reading. Saying bad things about the president or his family, or questioning the political order of the Maldives (which amounts to the same thing), are high on the list. This effectively curbs freedom of speech and people are very wary of getting into any kind of political discussion or expressing their opinions openly, even in private. Nor should the Prophet's name be taken in vain. Members of parliament cannot be prosecuted, however, for expressing their thoughts because what is said in the *Majlis*, is considered confidential.

Around 600 people are currently serving sentences on outlying outlands, 250 of whom are thought to be under house arrest as political prisoners. Prominent political offenders are sent to Dhoonidhoo, a small island just north of Malé where they can be billeted in the former residence of the British governor. In general, women suffer the worst as banishment is synomymous with the loss of social grace. In Maldivian terms, one becomes a scarlet women and an easy target for tom-catting village men. The experience can be ameliorated, though, for families often make arrangements for banished relatives to be fed and lodged by an island family. Wealthier criminals are free to make even more comfortable arrangements.

Several Westerners have suffered this unusual incarceration, being set down on a sparsely populated or uninhabited island with a few coconut palms and some government-supplied fish hooks with which to subsist. One was an American college student who tried to sell hashish to the police chief's son. The islanders, strict Muslims all, demanded he take refuge in the headman's house every time a native woman approached the tree under which he lived. A German who strangled his French girlfriend in 1976 fared better. He grew so fond of his personal exile on Fuludu island in Baa Atoll, that he kicked drugs and alcohol, according to local police. When the German ambassador flew in from Shri Lanka to tell him he could be deported back to Germany to complete his sentence, his answer was 'No thanks, I like it better here'. He has since converted to Islam and married a local woman.

Banishment has become so popular that at least three other Germans and a Swede have demanded to be punished for drug offences by being exiled in paradise. This method of visa extension is not recommended as the government favours the simpler solution of deporting troublesome aliens.

# Signs and Symbols

The national flag of the Maldives is a green rectangle, representing the universal colour of Islam, with a red border, which is the blood of the nation in sacrifice, with a white crescent in the centre, which is the symbol of the faith. The national emblem shows a coconut palm, crescent and star, and two crisscrossed national flags, plus the traditional title of state. The national tree is, of course, the coconut palm, and the national flower is the pink rose. While tourists would perhaps prefer a larger entry stamp in their passports as proud evidence of their visit to this beautiful country, the Maldives' postage stamps are large and decorative with sporting activities, marine life and fishing being popular themes.

# Malé

The tiny, saucer-shaped island capital of the Maldives is rarely more than a port of entry (and for most visitors, not even that). Malé—pronounced 'Mah-lee'—may have the distinction of being the largest island in the archipelago, but it is hardly a metropolis and the majority of visitors prefer to escape immediately to their island retreat, perhaps returning to the capital for a short excursion. To a visitor's eye, this administrative hamlet of coral-stone houses and sandy streets appears in a state of continual siesta. Squat, tannin-skinned fishermen wearing petticoat *lungis* shuffle through the coral dust down the main street carrying freshly caught tuna. The women leave a trace of coconut oil in the air as they waft past in long nylon or cotton dresses which cover their bodies in the burqa fashion with snippet-like veils, a relic from a brief period under Portuguese rule.

Taxi drivers blast out strains of 'Abba', the saccharine-sweet Swedish pop group, into the otherwise quiet streets. Meanwhile, the capital's cruisers ride the potholes high up in pick-up trucks, on the look out for unwary jaywalkers (who commit an offence by not crossing at designated places). The local boys collect scars from motorbike pile-ups, which are dainty affairs at the best of times because there's a 25 kph (15 mph) speed limit on the sand-blown main street. There are only 691 registered motor vehicles anyway, too few for the Maldivians to have got around to introducing car insurance, or to drop the need to register your bicycle with the authorities.

The smell of fish permeates everywhere. The waterfront is barely visited apart from a flurry of activity after the fishing catch is landed in the early hours of the morning. Indian Hindi film music wafts out of single-storey shopfronts selling imported Singaporean polyesters and thongs. Locals seem to have a fetish for imported lacy items, and plastic goods have the gleam of gold for young Maldivians. The kids hang out in several cafés, notably 'Quench' on Mijheedhee Magu.

A tangible lethargy hangs in the air with the embankment's salty wafts. Along the waterfront wild-eyed fishermen with stained gums lurk in tea shops, with names like 'Queen of the Night' and 'Beach Cafe', chewing betel wrapped in a leaf with coral lime and a stick of clove. Or they smoke *bidis* made of a single leaf of tobacco wrapped in old newspaper, of formidable strength and for all the world looking like huge reefers. An advertisement for an upcoming civic attraction listed 'Fairy Cocktails' at the local high school gym.

The unimposing building which houses the museum is partially hidden under shady mangosteen trees and the minaret of the main mosque, its first exhibit is a bullet-ridden Honda 125 from the last coup attempt in 1988. It also has a collection of pre-Buddhist statues dug up in the islands by Thor Heyerdahl.

I met the Attorney General, a rather avuncular man who had a theory that crime

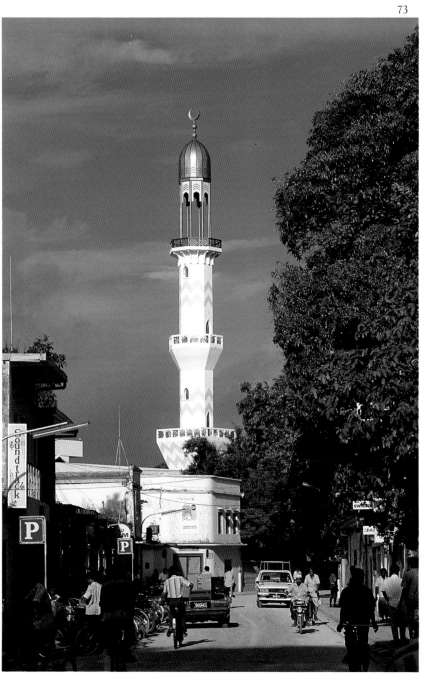

*The golden dome of the Grand Friday Mosque, Malé*

could be significantly reduced by getting people to eat large amounts of fish. Since no Maldivians have murdered each other for several decades, he did have a point. As the sun declines, evening joggers—members of the National Security Force not currently on duty—make a circuit of the island. Usually they stand, armed with automatic rifles, in front of the president's palace and the parliament building, the Majlis, with its peppermint colours and pastel tiles.

The *muezzin*'s mournful cry blares out across the flat roofs from tinny loudspeakers, organizing the last of the day's prayers for the Sunni faithful in the 40 or so mosques around the capital. Afterwards, the liveliest part of town is the evening fish market, overspilling with old detergent bottles filled with fish paste. It starts at six in the morning and finishes about nine in the evening, around the point of darkness. At dusk it fills up with the day's catch, with the largest fish, a swordfish, lying pellucid on a platter for inspection. Other foods grown in the Maldives include sweet potato, cassava, taro, the occasional cucumbers, spinach, sorghum, red onions, ridge gourds, bitter gourds, cabbages and chillies, all from the south. If you're lucky you may find watermelons from far-off Thoddu in Ari Atoll, or guavas, jujubes, custard and wood apples, or even sapodillas.

The kids are congregating in the milk shake bars again, concrete huts nestling under the arches of the football stadium on the main street, part of the big renovation made in the 1970s before the tourist boom took off. Water is sometimes in short supply. There are now five desalination plants with a capacity to produce 1,440 cubic metres of water per day. Malé used to have some 6,000 wells bored into the freshwater water-table that reached down 20 metres (66 feet) years ago, or at least it did in 1921 when the census put the population at 6,127. With almost 100 times that number 70 years later, the average depth of the water-table is only about 1.2 metres (3.6 feet), shallower than the trenches in the road. Coastal sea defences will keep out freak storm waves, but the freshwater level must rise as the sea-level rises so that Malé and all the Maldivian islands appear doomed to eventual extinction.

## Orientation

It is quite possible to walk from one end of Malé to the other in 20 minutes, so finding your way around the island is very straightforward. You'll need your map to navigate Malé's streets and alleys, however, since many are either in Dhivehi script or unmarked. It's useful to know that *magu* is the Maldivian word for a wide coral street, *goalhi* is a narrow alley, and a *higun* is a slightly longer and wider one.

The main centre of activity is Marine Drive, the harbour front strip that wraps itself halfway around the island from the north. The other principal streets are the north-south Chandani Magu and Majidi Magu, which divides it from east to west. The capital is divided into four districts—Maafannu, Machangolhi, Henveiru, and Galolhu—though you cannot notice much difference. Maafannu covers the northwestern end of the island from the Singapore bazaar area of Chandani Magu; it encloses the presidential residence, some of the foreign embassies, and many of Malé's guesthouses. Machangolhi runs east-west across the middle of the island and contains Malé's popular shopping strip, Majidi Magu. Galolhu is a crowded maze of coral-stone houses in the southeastern end of Malé, where you can see how most residents live. Henveiru in the north-eastern pocket of Malé encloses Ameer Ahmed Magu, where wealthier Maldivians live in slightly more elaborate villas on Marine Drive, overlooking the harbour. The reclaimed land is largely to the south, which is where activities such as go-downs, workshops and football pitches are concentrated. The fishing and cargo port is to the west of Chandani Magu; the tourist and yacht harbour to the east.

## THE ISLAMIC CENTRE

The huge, gold-domed, three-storey Islamic Centre, the island's most famous and most vivid architectural landmark with its 133 minarets, was declared open by President Gayoom in 1984. It houses an Islamic library, a conference hall, and classrooms, where a number of activities are conducted. Most important is the centrepiece Grand Mosque, named after Sultan Muhammad Thakurufaanu Al A'zam, which can shelter over 5,000 people. Its main prayer hall displays beautiful woodcarvings and Arabic calligraphy created by Maldivian craftsmen; four huge chandeliers and purpose-woven carpets add a glossy touch.

## HUKURU MISKIIY—THE FRIDAY MOSQUE

The Friday Mosque was built in 1656 during the reign of Sultan Ibrahim Iskandhar and stands on the site of the very first mosque in Malé. The exterior is built from coral stones fitted together along grooves, not with masonry. The interior is intricately carved with Arabic writings and woodcarvings in coconut, teak, sandalwood and mahogany relating the conversion of the Maldives to Islam. Coral carvings showing geometrical designs and local flora are quite unusual. Inside, the mosque has three *dhaalas*, raised platforms placed on all sides except the west. Inscriptions in Arabic and *dhives akuru* on the walls spell out duties of the imam. Twelve lacquered domes in the roof are covered with floral designs in bright colours of red, blue, green and gold.

Outside there are three wells within the compound walls for ritual ablutions. The

# Male

Indian Ocean

sundial is only about 70 years old and was used to calculate the five times of daily prayer. In a bid to preserve the mosque, the thatched roof and the western end was covered with corrugated iron in 1912, and aluminium in 1964, to prevent the sun's rays falling directly on the mosque, though this has somewhat marred the historic beauty of the building. The *munnaaru* minaret was erected in 1668 after the then sultan made the *hajj* pilgrimage to Mecca; it was renewed early this century with iron and copper bindings on the outside, replacing the old rope ones. Loudspeakers for the *mudhim*, the *muezzins*'s call to prayer, were installed in 1964 but are not used today.

The compound also includes a number of ancient tombstones, erected in memory of past kings, noblemen and heroes, including Sultan Ibrahim Iskander I who repulsed the Portuguese raid of 1649. A scholar, Sheik Ibrahim Rushdy, was also buried here some 30 years ago. The pointed stones indicate graves of men, the round ones, women's graves.

## Eid Miskiiy

Malé's second-oldest mosque is in the western part of the town. It was built in 1815 on the site of an earlier one using a design borrowed from the Friday Mosque.

## Medhu Ziyaarath

Opposite the Friday Mosque is the Medhu Ziyaarath, a shrine in memorial to Abul Barakaath-Al Barbarie, revered as the man who promoted the conversion of the Maldives to Islam in 1153. The white flag flown each Friday is a weekly commemoration of this heavily mythologized figure.

## Mulee-Aage—The Presidential Palace

This palace was built by Sultan Shamshuddin III in about 1913 for his son and heir, Al Ameer Hassan Izzaiyadheen. In 1936 he and his son were banished and their property forfeited to the government. It became the chief council house during the Second World War and location of the archipelago's first *maakoani* radio, which was used to listen to wartime broadcasts. When the republic was proclaimed in 1953, the palace became the president's official residence, and is famous for its nursery of rare plants. It was also the chief guesthouse, where visitors have included such illustrious foreign dignitaries as Queen Elizabeth II, the leader of the Palestinian Liberation Organization, Yasser Arafat, and former Indian Prime Minister, Mr Rajiv Gandhi. The site was historically the family home of the Huravee family, starting with Hassan Maniffaar, who expelled the Malabari invaders in the 15th century. The current building was designed by Sinhalese and Maldivian architects and reflects a colonial rather than an indigenous or Islamic influence. This doesn't explain the garish pastel tiles on the outside, which certainly look like a local fetish and can hardly be blamed on British colonialism. Subsequent governments used the palace to house state offices and made alterations to the official residence. In 1953, when the country became a republic for the second time, Mulee-Aage became the presidential palace.

## SULTAN PARK MUSEUM

The museum in the Sultan's Park used to be part of the old Royal Palace. It was seen by the French exile François Pyrard de Laval in the early 17th century but was destroyed by a Malabari invasion in 1752. The rest was destroyed in the 1960s, as the government at the time did not appreciate its historical value. Opened on the National Day, 1 Rabeeul Awwal 1372 AH (19 November 1952) by the then Prime Minister, Amir Mohamed Amin Didi, the museum is now a somewhat ramshackle building which houses various interesting artefacts, watched over by a covey of old men.

Two of the most important items exhibited are a coral stone head of a statue of Lord Buddha and a wooden panel erected in the Hukuru Miskiiy (Friday Mosque) in 737 AH. The head of Lord Buddha, amongst other similar objects, indicates that Buddhism existed in the Maldives before conversion to Islam, while the panel, which is about four metres long, bears an Arabic inscription that gives the date of conversion to Islam.

The cannon outside is a legacy of the Portuguese occupation that ended in 1573 (others can be seen in different places along Malé's waterfront, not quite cleared away and absorbed into the landscape). Relics from Thor Heyerdahl's expedition lie in a corner, as yet unlabelled, in a disorganized rubble of sandstone and coral. Most were found in the southernmost islands, including Ari Atoll, and all date prior to the Maldives' 12th-century conversion to Islam, which perhaps explains their state of semi-benign neglect. The Buddha head from Kurendhu in Lhaviyani Atoll was found in 1962. Pride of place goes to the three-metre-high (ten feet) head from Thoddu. Mundu island has provided some carved lions and a monkey's head.

The rest of the museum is chock-a-block with odds and ends. A random selection gives the flavour of the collection, bizarre yet curiously fascinating: the decrepit first printing press sent to the Maldives; palanquins used by the last sultan in 1932; a photograph of the moon by Neil Armstrong; and an old sand-glass egg timer. One of my favourites is a newspaper cutting by an early travel writer, one C W Rossett, from a London illustrated magazine, *The Graphic*, dated 1886, and showing a plump girl idling in a swinging chair with the caption 'this the chief amusement of Maldives women'. Elsewhere, the antiquarian will be pleased by examples of the old script *dhives akuru* engraved on a wooden plank and dating from the 13th century, and old coins dating from 1620, showing the progression from coins shaped like little pins instead of being round, to recognizable circular money. At the modern end there's a vast range of mouldering ceremonial attire, embroidered coats that belonged to the sultans' womenfolk, ghoulish sepia photographs, silver ornaments, letters from colonial visitors, 18th-century turbans, lacquer trays used for a sultan's special holiday food, tin drum-holders used to sound imperial gongs, knives and sundry seals, prayer carpets, broken model boats, and rickety umbrellas made of cotton and used to shade the sun's rays from the sultan's eyes. More poignant are the two bullet-ridden motorbikes, on which a lance-corporal in the security forces was killed in the brief crossfire during the 1988 disturbances. A sarong used by the nation's saviour, Thakurafaanu, is the most valuable item, and the oldest. The museum is open daily from 9.00 am to 3.00 pm, except on Fridays and public holidays.

## Esjehi Gallery

Esjehi Gallery was opened 26 October 1991. The gallery's aim is to develop art in the country by holding different exhibitions every month on vernacular architecture and contemporary art. This gallery is located in a century-old building and is open daily (except Fridays) from 9.00 am to 1.30 pm and from 2.00 pm to 7.00 pm. It is well worth visiting.

(Left and above) *Stone sculpture and traditional textiles, National Museum, Malé*

## BIHUROAZU KAMANAA MISKIIY

The tomb of Mohammed Thakurufaanu, the Maldivian hero who defeated the occupying Portuguese and restored the country's independence, lies in the compound of this mosque. He died in 1585.

## ALI RASGEFAANU ZIYAARATH

Although Sultan Ali VI, popularly known as Ali Rasgefaanu, ruled the country for only two and a half months, his place in Maldivian history is secure as one of the country's greatest heroes. He died in 1558 while defending the homeland from Portuguese mercenaries. The tombstone marks the exact spot in the sea where the sultan fell after being hit by an enemy arrow. Then it stood in knee-deep water, but recent reclamation has brought the memorial site onto dry land.

# Malé Directory

## Hotels and Guesthouses

Do not fall into the trap of looking for a place to stay during the peak season without booking well in advance, as there is so little space it will use up a lot of the time you could be spending on the beach or on a boat. The main hotels in Malé are often block-booked by aid agencies for staffers working on development projects in the Maldives. The two main areas in which to look for accommodation are to the left of the main jetty as you arrive on Marine Drive, and in the central area. Expect to pay a lot for what you get if you want anything above the most basic room for the night. Food is generally pretty poor.

### EXPENSIVE

**Alia Hotel**, Haveeree Higun . Tel. 32–2080, 3445, 2935; tlx. 77032 HOTALIA MF (airconditioned rooms, s/d $40–54; with fans). Renovations are currently being undertaken.

**Nasandhura Palace Hotel**, Marine Drive. Tel. 32–3380 (5 lines); fax. 32–0822; tlx. 66019 POLYCOM MF. The marine-front location is convenient for late-night arrivals or early morning departures to and from the airport. A spartan two-storey block which is far from palatial, but it is the best hotel in Malé. The restaurant has an à la carte menu. The bar is a favourite with Malé's tiny expatriate community who linger here virtually all day to down Heineken and Singapore Lion beer and evening cocktails, an oasis in an otherwise alcohol-free Malé. Airconditioned rooms, s/d $55–75.

### MODERATE

**Buruneege**, tel. 32–2870.
**Gaadhoo**, tel. 32–3222.
**Lifshaam**, tel. 32–5386.
**Maagiri Tourist Lodge**, tel. 32–2576.
**Meedhu**, tel. 32–4970.
**Sakeena Menzil**, tel. 32–3281.
**Sony Guest House**, tel. 32–3249.

### AT THE WEST END OF MALÉ IN MAAFANNU
**Kaimoo**, tel. 32–3241.
**Fehividhuvaruge**, tel. 32–3241.
**Malé Tour Inn**, tel. 32–6220.
**Mermaid Inn**, tel. 32–3329.
**Ocean Reed**, tel. 32–3311.
**Transit Lodge**, tel. 32–6516.
**Travel Inn Tourist Lodge**, tel. 32–6528.

### AT THE THE SOUTHERN END, IN GALOLHU
**Beach Travel Lodge II**, tel. 32–5966.
**Grace Inn**, tel. 32–0540.
**Selvio**, tel. 32–4671.
**Tetra**, tel. 32–3305.

(following pages) *Marine Drive, Malé*

In the central area of Machchangolhi
Araarootuge Guesthouse, tel. 32–2661.
Kosheege, tel. 32–3585.
Marvel Rest, tel. 32–6294.
Mazaage, tel. 32–4669.

At the northern end, in Henveiru
Aahama Guest House, tel. 32–3133.
Beach Travel Tourist Lodge,
tel. 32–0092.
Keesa Guest House, tel. 32–2508.
Noofaru, tel. 32–2731.
Reedhoo Kokaa, tel. 32–2505.
Sun Rise Lodge, tel. 32–1501.
Zoneyria Guest House, tel. 32–3298.

## Restaurants

Bamboo, near the Customs Building. Currently a guesthouse charging $35 night. Its French owner serves French, Creole, and Italian food. Tel. 32–3241.

Beach Café, downtown at the intersection of Madji Magu and Marine Drive. Open 9.00 am to 1.00 am. Maldivian and European-style, milkshakes and snacks, including the exotic *dhonkeyo kajuru* made of deep-fried bananas.

Cheers, Dhaburuh Magu, opposite the Malé English school, this is a snack bar and caterer. Tel. 32–8654.

Dragon, located on the eastern Marine Drive, this is a Thai restaurant. Tel. 32–2009.

Intime, at the northern Marine Drive near the State Bank of India, serves continental dishes and provides a delivery service. Tel. 32–1737.

Queen of the Night, Marine Drive, and The Tea Shop, Ameer Ahmed Magu. Two rough and ready fishermen's hangouts with very cheap Maldivian snacks and endless cups of tea.

Quench, centrally located at Majeedhee Magu, continental and western food. Tel. 32–4571.

Slice, at the main shopping area on Faamudheryi Magu, serves snacks and continental dishes. Tel. 32–0566.

Scoop, at Chandhani Magu, serves ice cream specialities. Tel. 32–2422.

Twin Peaks, Mafannu on Orchid Magu, replacing Tiffany's, continental and western food served. Tel. 32–7830.

## Shopping

Duty Free Paradise, Umar Shopping Arcade, Chandani Magu. Tel. 32–3864.
Palm Duty Free, Umar Shopping Arcade, Chandani Magu.

# Taxis

**Comfort Taxi Fare**, tel. 32–8998, (24-hours).
**Dialacab**, tel. 32–3132 (24-hours).
**Khaleej Taxi**, tel. 32–5060 (24-hours).
**Kulee Dhuveli**, tel. 32–2122 (24-hours).
**Lunghi Taxi Service**, tel. 32–5454.
**New Taxi Service**, tel. 32–5757 (24-hours).
**Regular Taxi Service Co**, tel. 32–2454.

# Medical Services

**Malé's Central Hospital** has 84 beds and is on the corner of Sosun Magu and Majeedhee Magu. Tel. 32–2400.

**The Indira Gandhi Memorial Hospital** nearing completion will have 200 beds. Dispensaries can be found on Sosun Magu and on Majeedee Magu, opposite the football stadium; there are 26 in all. Thirty doctors (13 general duty and 17 specialists) are available. They all speak English.

# Airline Offices

**Air Lanka**
Ameer Ahmed Magu. Tel. 32–3459. Daily flights to Colombo.

**Air Maldives**
Marine Drive. Tel. 32–2436.

**Emirates Airlines**
Marine Drive. Tel. 32–4591. Three flights weekly to Dubai.

**Indian Airlines**
H Sifaa, Marine Drive. Tel. 32–3003. Three flights weekly to Trivandrum.

**Singapore Airlines**
MHA Building, 2/Fl, Orchid Magu. Tel. 32–0777. Six flights weekly.

**Pakistan International Airways**
Luxwood #1 Marine Drive. Tel. 32–3532. Twice weekly to Karachi.

# Airline Representatives

**Alitalia**
c/o Air Maldives, Marine Drive. Tel. 32–5676.

**Austrian Airlines/Condor**
Universal Travel Dept, 18 Marine Drive. Tel. 32–3116.

**Emirates Airlines**
Marine Drive. Tel. 32–4591. Three flights weekly to Dubai.

**Eva Air**
Universal Enterprises, 38 Orchid Magu, Tel. 32–2971.

**Lauda Air**
Fantasy Trade & Travels Ltd, Fareedhee Magu. Tel. 32–4668.

Royal Nepalese Airlines
Speed Travels, Fareedhee Magu.
Tel. 32–3069.

Sterling Airways/Balair/Zas
Voyages Maldives Pvt Ltd, 2 Fareedhee
Magu. Tel. 32–2019.

Habib Bank Ltd
1/6 Orchid Magu. Tel. 32–2051.

Maldives Monetary Authority
Chandhani Magu. Tel. 32–2291.

State Bank of India
H Zonaria, Marine Drive. Tel. 32–3053.

# Government Ministries

# High Commissions

Department of Immigration &
Emigration
2/Fl Huravee Bldg, Ameeru Ahmed
Magu. Tel. 32–3913.

Department of Information & Broad-
casting
3/Fl Huravee Bldg, Ameeru Ahmed
Magu. Tel. 32–3837.

Ministry of Atolls Administration
Faashanaa Bldg, Marine Drive.
Tel. 32–2826, 3070.

Ministry of Tourism
2/Fl Ghaazee Bldg, Ameer Ahmed Magu.
Tel. 32–3224, 3596; fax 32–2512;
tlx. 66019 TOURISM MF.

Indian High Commision
Maafaanu Aage. Tel. 32–3716.

Pakistani High Commission
2 Moonimaage. Tel. 32–3005.

Shri Lankan High Commission
H Sakeena Manzil. Tel. 32–2845.

# Honorary Consuls

Bangladesh
Mohammed Umar Manik, Universal
Enterprises, 38 Orchid Magu.
Tel. 32–3080.

Denmark/Sweden
Abdulla Saeed, Cyprea, 25 Marine Drive.
Tel. 32–2451.

# Banks

Bank of Ceylon
Orchid Magu. Tel. 32–3046.

Bank of Maldives
Marine Drive. Tel. 32–2948.

France
Mohamed Ismail Manik, 1/27 Chandhani
Magu. Tel. 32–4132.

**USA**
Midhath Hilmy, Mandhuedhuruge, Violet Magu. Tel. 32–2581.

No other countries have diplomatic or consular representatives in the Maldives.

# Tour and Resort Operators

The following companies organize a wide range of tours, boat trips, diving safaris, cruises on yacht-*dhonis*, and inter-island boat and speedboat transfers. Some also operate resorts and hotels; they can certainly quote and arrange stays at resorts. The major companies are ZSS and Voyages Maldives, but the smaller companies also have suitable cruising boats of different sizes for hire.

**AAA & Trading Co**
Chandhani Magu. Tel. 32–4487.

**Akir**
Marine Drive. Tel. 32–2719, 2592; fax. 32–3463; tlx. 77065 HOLIDAY MF.

**Akiri Enterprises**
Marine Drive. Tel. 32–2719; tlx. 77074 MAKANA MF.

**Altaf Enterprises Ltd, 8 Majeedi Bazaar.**
Tel. 32–2890, 3378; tlx. 66047 ALTAF MF.

**Beach Travel & Tours**
1/10 Ameer Ahmed Magu. Tel. 32–4572.

**Cyprea Ltd, 25 Marine Drive.**
Tel. 32–2451; fax. 32–3523.

**Deens Orchid Agency**
2/11 H Marine Drive. Tel. 32–2844, 8005, 7450; fax. 32-3779.

**Detours**
Fasmeeru, Hulangubai  Marine Drive. Tel. 32–1806; fax. 32–7079.

**Discovery Tours (Pvt) Ltd**
13 Orchid Magu. Tel. 32–3975.

**Dhirham Travels & Chandling**
Faamudheyri Magu. Tel. 32–3369; tlx. 77050 VALTUR MF

**Dolphin Enterprises Ltd**
G.Makhumaage. Tel. 32–4445; tlx. 66081 DOLPHIN MF.

**Eurasia Agencies**
Meduziyaaraiy Magu. Tel. 32–4538

**Express**
Tel. 32–2432.

**Fantasy Trade & Travels**
3/2 Fareedhee Magu. Tel. 32–4668; tlx. 66078 Fantasy MF.

**Fun Tours Trade and Travel**
M Muniyaavilla. Tel. & fax. 32–4459.

**Galena Maldives (Pte) Ltd**
Orchid Magu. Tel. 32–4742/3;
fax. 32–4465.

**Golden Jet Trade & Travels Ltd**
13 Chandhani Magu. Tel. 32–2338;
tlx. 77095 ARIMALÉ MF.

**Imad's Agencies**
Jawahiriyya, Chandhani Magu.
Tel. 32–3441; fax. 32–6924;

**Jetan Travels**
Marine Drive. Tel. 32–4628.

**Kaimoo Travels**
Roanunge. Tel. 32–2212; tlx. 66035
KAIMOO MF.

**Maldivian Traders & Contracting**
Tel. 32–2828, 2807–8. Two hovercraft
and eight launches.

**Nazaki Services**
Tel. 32–4314/5.

**Olympia**
1/Fl Ahmadhee Bazaar. Tel. 32–2037,
3021; tlx. 66094 OLMPIA MF.

**Phoenix Travel Pvt Ltd**
Fasmeeru Hulhagubai. Tel 32–3587; tlx.
77080 PHOENIX MF.

**Quest Enterprises**
H Hickory. Tel. 32–3014.

**Remses Travel Service**
Henveiru, Malé. Tel. 32–2854/5;
tlx. 77024 REMSIS MF

**Safari Tours**
1 Chandhani Magu. Tel. 32–3524; fax.
32–2516; tlx. 66030 SAFARI MF.

**Sea Coast**
Marine Drive. Tel. 32–3364;
tlx. 66021 VCZ MALÉ MF.

**Speed Travels**
Faridi Magu. Tel. 32–4280.

**Sunland Travel (Pvt) Ltd**
Finihiyaa Goalhi. Tel. 32–4685; fax 32–
5543; tlx. 77064 SUNLAND MF.

**Suntour Maldives**
4 Marine Drive. Tel. 32–3467; fax 32–
3466; tlx. 77065 HOLIDAY MF.

**Treasure Island Enterprises**
8 Marine Drive. Tel. 32–3531;
fax. 32–5645.

**Universal Enterprises**
38 Orchid Magu. Tel. 32–2971, 3080;
fax. 32–2678; tlx. 66024 UNIENT MF.

**Voyage Maldives**
2 Fareedhee Magu. Tel. 32–3617; fax.
32–5336; tlx. 66063 VOYAGE MF.

**ZSS**
5 Fiyaathoshi Goalhi, Henveiru.
Tel. 32–2505, 3505; fax. 32–4744;
tlx. 66020 ZSS MF.

# Air Transport

**Hummingbird Helicopters Pvt Ltd,**
MHA Building, 4/Fl, Orchid Magu. Tel.
32–5708; fax. 32–3161. This British
company runs a fleet of Sikorskys with
picture windows to helipads in Ari,
North Malé, South Malé and Lhavyani
Atolls, servicing 40 resorts.

# Festivals and Holidays

Friday is the national day of prayer and
rest; no public practice of religion other
than Islam.

### STATE HOLIDAYS ARE AS FOLLOWS:

| | |
|---|---|
| January 1 | New Year's Day |
| July 26 | Independence Day, from the British in 1965 |
| November 3 | Victory Day, over the terrorist attack in 1988 |
| November 11 | Republic Day, foundation in 1968 |

### OTHER CELEBRATIONS:

| | |
|---|---|
| National Day | On the first day of Rabee-ul-Awal, victory over the Portuguese in 1578 |
| Martyr's Day | Death of Sultan Ali VI at the hands of Portuguese in 1558 |

Dhonis *which ply the waters between the islands*

| | | | |
|---|---|---|---|
| Huravee Day | Defeat of the Malabaris in 1752 | Eid-ul-Fitr/Kuda Id | New moon after Ramadan, feast with sweets and relaxation |
| February | Opening of the *Majlis* (parliament) | Eid al Azha | Two months and ten days later |

RELIGIOUS FESTIVALS:

| | | | |
|---|---|---|---|
| February–March | Ramadan | July–August | Birthday of the Prophet Muhammad |
| Muslim New Year | First day of Shav val, first month of the Muslim calendar | | |

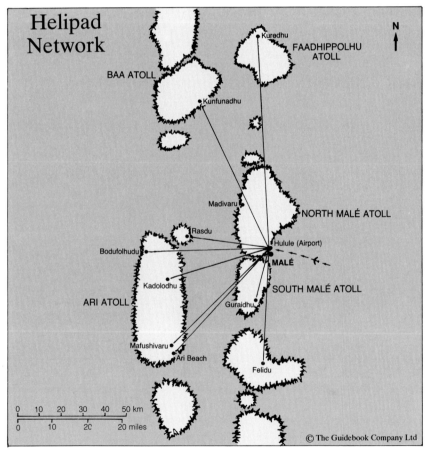

Helipad Network

N

BAA ATOLL

Kuredhu

FAADHIPPOLHU ATOLL

Kunfunadhu

Madivaru

NORTH MALÉ ATOLL

Rasdu

Hulule (Airport)

Bodufolhudu

MALÉ

Kadolodhu

SOUTH MALÉ ATOLL

ARI ATOLL

Guraidhu

Mafushivaru

Ari Beach

Felidu

| 0 | 10 | 20 | 30 | 40 | 50 km |
|---|---|---|---|---|---|
| 0 | | 10 | | 20 | 20 miles |

© The Guidebook Company Ltd

# Other Information

**American Express**
C/o Universal Enterprises, 8 Marine
Drive. Tel. 32–3116, 3166; fax. 32–2695.

**DHL**
C/o Cyprea Ltd, 25 Marine Drive.
Tel. 32-2451; fax. 32–3523.

**National Library**
59 Majeedi Magu. Open 9.00 am–noon
and 2.00 pm–5.00 pm except Ramadan
and Fridays. Tel. 32–3943–5.

**National Museum**
Open 9.00 am–3.00 pm except Fridays
and public holidays.

**Novelty Bookshop**
Fareedhee Magu. Tel. 32–2564.

**Skypak**
Deens Orchid Agency, Marine Drive.
Tel. 32–3779; fax. 32–3877; tlx. 77061
ORCHID MF.

# The Great Parade

I landed in Male on a Monday, and on the Friday following I went to see the Sultan's procession returning from the Jama Masjid after prayers. Friday among Moslems is observed in the same manner as Sunday with Christians and the first portion of the day is reserved for prayer.

I left the house about one o'clock as I was told that prayers would finish about half-past one. The streets seemed quite deserted and silent and every shop and little boutique was closed.

The whole atmosphere reminded me of nothing so much as a small township or village in the the north of Scotland on a Sunday. This effect was further heightened by the fact that it was a dull grey day with heavy rain clouds working up from the south-west.

I posted myself at a corner near the high-walled palace of the Sultan which commanded a good view of the approach to the mosque. After a time two men with reddish check turbans, bare to the waist and wearing dark brown sarongs with two broad stripes at the foot and edged with white strolled past. These I was told were the nucleus of the band and some had gone to fetch the drums. Later a figure all in white wearing a long flowing Arab jibbah and white turban walked past in a stately manner. This was the Khatib or High Priest himself who had just finished prayers. Except for the turban he might have been the photographic negative of a Scotch Minister leaving the kirk without doffing his black Geneva gown. The Mullah even wore what appeared very like a round starched collar which closely resembled the regulation ecclesiastical "dog collar". He was followed by another white-robed figure carrying a parcel wrapped in a dark silk cloth which contained the Koran Sharif and other devotional books. Then appeared some men in white coats or blouses edged with black, with black shoulder straps and black piping on the sleeves. On the head was a small red cap attached to a light chain. These were members of the Police Force or Civil Guard.

Shortly after, about forty of the Sultan's lashkar or Guards lined up on either side of the road, the leader or colour-sergeant bearing a white furled *flag. They all wore check turbans, were bare to the waist and wore the same kind of sarong as the bandsmen, only the colour was dark blue instead of brown. Half of them were armed with lances and the remainder with what looked like very ancient muzzle loaders.*

*In the waist cloth of each could be seen the ivory handle, in some cases mounted in silver work, of a dagger much resembling an Arab* jambir, *or Persian* khanjar. *The sheaths had ornamental silk tassels at the tip. There was a fanfare of trumpets which heralded the trumpeters with long brass instruments. They were immediately followed by two men with what are known on the Indian frontier as a* saranai—*a kind of clarinet. The moment the trumpets ceased the clarinets burst forth in a weird minor strain. They were accompanied by three drummers, each bearing what is called in India a* dhol *or large drum and a* beru *by the Maldivians. This is beaten with both hands.*

*Then came a young man, the nephew of the Sultan, who represented him. Close behind and on either side of him were two umbrella bearers. One of the umbrellas was the white State one used only by the Sultan or his representative, whilst the other was of a delicate rose colour. Both had gilded tops and were elaborately frilled.*

*The young man wore over a* jibbah *of dark green a* saduriya *or waistcoat of salmon colour and had a tarbush on his head. He looked neither to his right nor his left but straight ahead and passed through the gateway leading to the palace.*

*The Sultan does not himself always attend Friday prayers, and on this occasion neither the Prince nor the Prime Minister were present as both were indisposed.*

*The last I saw of the procession as it disappeared through the gate was the umbrellas being twirled around rapidly over the representative's head.*

T W Hockly, The Two Thousand Isles, *1935*

# Choosing a Resort

There are now more than 69 purpose-built tourist resorts in the Maldives, and after a lull in the late 1980s more are coming onstream every year. Tourist development in the archipelago has growth rings as obvious as those of trees. The most established, and often the most popular resorts, are centred around Malé in the North Malé Atoll. A second group spread in the late 1970s throughout South Malé Atoll. The present wave of expansion is taking place in Ari Atoll, where many new resorts opened during the 1991–92 season. Vaavu Atoll has also opened two resorts. The authorities are sure they are on the right track keeping tourists basically segregated from the indigenous population and pushing resorts further up-market by making the terms of their leases more stringent. Many resorts are being renovated and upgraded as their leases come up for renewal or as the market changes, most recently because of an influx of Japanese tourists with higher expectations. Resorts that have expanded and upgraded recently include Kurumba, Kanifinolhu, Bandos, Bodhufinolhu, Kuredhdhu, Kuramathi, Vaadhu, and Lhohifushi.

There is little danger that the Maldives will become heavily over-exploited as has happened with other tourist destinations like Pattaya in Thailand, or parts of Bali in Indonesia. For one thing, the government is concerned to isolate foreigners from the locals, something which a massive, uncontrolled influx would jeopardize. It is keen to keep that 'quality feel' for as long as the country's stretched resources can cope. Secondly, the Maldives can offer the best of one type of holiday: a sea and sun resort-style vacation with the chance to learn a new sport thrown in, in waters that are among the top three diving grounds in the world. It has none of the other cultural attractions (or, in the case of Pattaya, sleazy sexploitation) that travellers associate with Asia. Thus it continues to attract a hard core of water sports enthusiasts and honeymooners rather than singles or families. Many resorts, notably the smaller ones, report high return rates, often year after year.

The country also appeals to the newest generation of travel spenders, the Japanese, who love the combination of pristine beaches, convivial company—often of fellow honeymooners—and laid-on activities in a theme environment. The government says it is planning to take back some of the resort islands to house the ever-growing local population, a move which is becoming more important as overcrowding increases in Malé. However, this is not certain as the tourist dollar is a vital and stable form of income; a few islands that can be absorbed easily may change, but not many more.

As everywhere, though, you get what you pay for and there's sufficient range to make it worth carefully considering your priorities (and your budget). With the exception of a few very exclusive resorts, most islands are not noted for their solitude or privacy. You will almost certainly be isolated on a tiny island for your holiday, but in the peak season you are likely to be joined by up to 100 or so other tourists. Many of the best resorts are practically block booked by an agent with a particular style or nationality of clientele, so your choice is often predetermined by those listed in your own country's brochures.

Choose your island with care. Many people go to another island for a second visit to the archipelago only to be disappointed that their second choice wasn't as good as their first. The best of the Maldives costs quite a lot to enjoy, but in most cases it is worth it. Several places, however, claim to be much more than they really are, and have prices to match. Others give the impression of being probably quite dreadful, the advance warning, perhaps, of mass tourism that is so far only mildly evident. A few, notably the Italian and Japanese resorts, cater so carefully for their clients that it would be a pleasure for almost anyone to experience them. If you feel like being private, you can be in the Maldives. You can also learn to windsurf or scuba dive, and are guaranteed a good tan in the space of a fortnight in the right season, when northern latitudes are swathed in winter.

Accommodation is generally in thatched cottages or bungalows, with an attached bathroom containing a bath and/or shower and a small veranda usually facing the sea and overlooking the beach. It's unusual to find any building higher than a single storey; only a half-dozen resorts have even a two-storey building on their islands. You don't have to move very far up-market to find detached accommodation that offers an extra degree of seclusion and comfort. This guide stresses such resorts, but even the spartan places can be appealing as a way to 'get away from it all'.

Practically every resort offers a range of outdoor facilities that includes diving, snorkelling, sailing, water-skiing, parasailing, and catamaran sailing. Other activities, sometimes outdoors, sometimes indoors in special gymnasia (the latest indication of the upwardly mobile resort) include volleyball, badminton, tennis, table tennis and aerobics. Almost all resorts can organize other activities such as day and night-time fishing excursions. On the social side, all the large resorts offer modern attractions like a disco floor, evening videos, cultural shows, island hopping tours, a souvenir shop, and sedentary board games. All of them have a tiny mosque in the compound for the local workers, just to remind you that you aren't in a completely rootless paradise.

Visitors tend to have two main complaints: food and fresh water. The food can be bland and uninspiring in some resorts. This is more true in the larger ones which find it hard to cook for several hundred guests at the same time, while relying even partially on local supplies for fresh produce. They all have to import large amounts of recognizably packaged western food to complement what is available locally. Smaller resorts can do much better, and indeed offer some of the best seafood you can find in

Asia, but the larger resorts do tend to have a lot of eating outlets, providing a wider choice of food than the smaller resorts.

Remember that water rarely cools properly in the tropics. It is difficult to get soap to lather, and shampoo can't do its job well, leaving you with a head of sticky, stiff hair. In the past, almost all the resorts used to pump water from the ground and filter it through the sand. The resulting water is quite unpleasant, even when boiled. To combat this, almost all the resorts now have desalinization plants, something that is now seen as a necessity; others collect fresh rainwater in barrels as a supplement. Some will provide fresh water 24 hours a day, while others restrict it to a few hours in the morning or evening. Occasionally the desalinization system breaks down or there are long periods without rain; then it's back to the bore hole water and sea water. It's probably better not to care too much, but hot water can be sorely missed even on a desert island. Visitors will find, however, that there are always flasks of bottled drinking water in rooms and at meals.

## Resorts Versus Cruising

Free and independent travellers are not encouraged to roam around the Maldives. It is not impossible to do so, but it is far from easy and only a certain type of person would feel the need to journey like this in the Maldives compared with, say, Indonesia which would repay such endeavours to a much greater extent. Back in the early 1980s a few hippie travellers made it here, though it was never quite on the trail which paused at Goa en route to Bali. However, in 1985, the government tightened things up and introduced a permit system which made it impossible to stay anywhere that's inhabited outside of Malé and not a resort, without getting permission first (though paradoxically it still seems you're free to use uninhabited islands as you please). A bed tax was established and all the guesthouses were closed down. Permission, which is granted by the Inter-Atolls Administration, is hard to get without a bona fide reason. One way out is to go by boat and to stay on board; the bed tax is levied anyway, but no one is going to cast you adrift at night.

Have a second look at the special section on organizing a cruise (page 36). This is the only real alternative to a prebooked and packaged resort holiday. Check the list of tour operators (page 90). They can advise on the types of boats available (generally you can stop over at resorts to pick up essential supplies, like drinks, in the evenings). If you like your freedom, the feeling of thrusting across the bluest of blue oceans, looked after by a skilled and sinewy Maldivian crew, is hard to match. Even if you have a language problem, they will help you choose an itinerary which the boat can manage in the time available and given the prevailing weather. The European operators listed will provide a more comfortable service in many ways, but are mainly busy servicing diving groups willing to pay the extra to get to new dive sites. Study the prices. If there is a group of you, it can work out cheaper to stay afloat and it really does provide an unforgettable escape if you are the kind of person who can't stay still on a beach for a week or ten days.

The next big growth area will probably be big-game fishing, as practised in Florida and on the Great Barrier Reef. The Maldives' no-net-trawling rule means that the big surface-fighting fish just get bigger: yellowfin tuna up to 270 kilos (600 pounds), swordfish and sailfish around 70 kilos (150 pounds), black marlin up to 635 kilos (1,400 pounds).

Finally, think about taking in another country on the way out or back, a diversion that your travel agent can very easily arrange. Shri Lanka is astonishingly beautiful and largely devoid of tourists in recent years; cheap air tickets are also available on the national airline, Air Lanka.

# Description of Resorts

The following pages describe all the resorts currently open to tourists in the Maldives. When choosing a resort, look carefully at the brochures issued by travel companies and carefully compare the facilities on offer against those listed here. You can get a pretty good feel for the resorts by the way they describe themselves in this literature as they always want to stress their best points; scrutinize the pictures closely, too.

You will need to consider several criteria when selecting the best resort for your own needs. A standard resort might be just what you're looking for, or simply what you can afford for the type of holiday you want. Whatever your choice, don't forget that the archipelago contains places of outstanding natural beauty, the like of which would be hard to find outside the remotest of Pacific islands. Look forward to the sight of an endless horizon, radiant waters, and a crisp, clear sky in twenty different shades of blue from sparklingly transparent to the deepest azure. The Maldives manages to combine that beauty with relatively easy access, especially if you are coming from Europe, in a pristine environment perfect for water sports.

Room rates shown here were in effect during the 1991–2 season. Slight increases can be expected, especially in the light of rising petroleum prices which affect transportation and electricity generation costs. All prices quoted are in US dollars per day per room. There is a wide variation between the rates quoted given by the resorts

## Cowrie Currency

The tiny cowrie shell turned the Maldives into a focus of international activity long before tourists were ever invented. The shell of *Cypraea moneta*, the money cowrie, was used in the lands bordering the Indian Ocean as a currency for over 3,000 years, and at least until the end of the 17th century. The archipelago served as a kind of mint for the entire region, a fact witnessed by Arab merchants 1,000 years ago as they began their expansion southwards in a bid to take over these lucrative trade routes. The legendary traveller, Ibn Battuta, visited the Maldives in 1343 and noted how the islanders cultivated cowries by putting palm leaves on the water's surface so that the molluscs would attach themselves. Then they dragged the leaves ashore and buried them in pits along the beach, so that the flesh would rot and leave only the bleached shells. He relates how the Maldivians sold them to Yemeni traders to serve as ballast, to Bengalis for rice, and to West Africans (by way of Amsterdam) at an exchange rate on a par with gold.

A Chinese chronicler who came with Cheng Ho's expedition to the Indian Ocean in 1433, tells how the cowries circulated in Bengal and Thailand. The Portuguese navigator, Vasco da Gama, found them when he came at the turn of the 15th century and tried to wrest the monopoly away from the Arabs. The shipwrecked Frenchman, François Pyrard de Laval, witnessed 40 ships leaving fully laden in 1611. Instances of use in China, central Finland, and East Africa show how far the trade routes went.

The cowries succumbed to two influences at about the same time: marauding Portuguese adventurers who disrupted the apparently efficient open-port system that prevailed in nearby Calicut and elsewhere in the region, and the arrival of the first coins around 1600, which put paid to the wild fluctuations in the cowries' value depending on the particular region in which it was traded. As recently as 90 years ago, the historian H C P Bell

themselves and the prices a travel agent can get for you. Tour operators offer a discount of up to 40 per cent on listed prices and everything is discretionary during the off-season, ie outside of the November–April high season, with discounts averaging 25 per cent. Some resorts halve their rates out of season, others only shave them. Talk to the operators direct, or to a local agent if you want to find out an accurate recounts that men on Isdu had to pay the sultan a tax of 18,000 cowries annually for themselves and a wife.

Almost all of our knowldge of Maldivian history comes from a chronicle called the *Ta'rikh*, compiled by the scholar Hasan Taj al-Din. This Arabic manuscript relates the story from the conversion of the first sultan, al-Malik al-'Adil Muhammad, up to the mid-19th century, almost 700 years of history. A complete copy was presented to the British in Colombo and then lost, though the monograph by H C P Bell, a former British Commissioner who first visited the islands in 1879, shows that he had seen it. Several versions written at other times have been found by a Japanese scholar in Malé.

Mention of the Maldives is made in sixth-century Alexandrian chronicles which placed it as one of the 1,370 islands adjacent to the largest of all islands, Taprobane, which we now call India. Arabic and Persian words entered the language, evidence of cross-fertilization from the north, as Tamil words are from the east. Other ancient scripts relate evidence of Maldivian participation in the *Hajj* pilgrimage to Mecca, and of the migration and exchange of reformist sufis and mullahs across the Indian Ocean. It is mentioned extensively in the travel books of Ibn Battuta, and a host of other Arabic travellers like al-Biruni, al-Idrisi, al-Dimashqi, and Ibn Majid.

It appears clear that the first recorded king of the Maldives was known as Prince Koimala who came to the country with his wife, the daughter of the king of Shri Lanka, in the early twelfth century. Contemporary Chinese chronicles call the area 'Three thousand weak waters', a reference dating back to the fifth century BC. It appears that the Maldives' conversion to Islam took place over a period of at least 70 years. Rulers of the outlying atolls resisted the change, but by the early 13th century the new religion had taken root and the succession of 84 sultans in six dynasties had begun.

price. Many are reluctant to reveal their Fixed Individual Tariff, the rate that applies to people who just turn up on the night (not an easy thing to do in the Maldives anyway). Package deals work out much cheaper and are by far the most popular way of arranging a holiday in the Maldives. It is very unwise to arrive without a booking since you may be disappointed by not getting accommodation in your chosen resort.

*(following pages) A helicopter ride provides spectacular aerial views*

# The Atolls

The 26 atolls of the Maldives are spread out across several hundred miles and grouped for convenience into 19 administrative groups. They have long names that are hard to pronounce, but the government has helpfully made it easier by listing them alphabetically running from north to south. Most people therefore identify the atoll group from the assigned letter of the Roman alphabet, from A to S. The same system is used for boat registration throughout the archipelago, so if you want to know where a boat is going to, or where it is from, look for the single letter painted on the prow. Since most *dhonis* ply between their own atoll and Malé this is a good way of choosing which *dhoni* to approach if you want to get a ride. Good luck!

## North Thiladhunmathi—A

At the farthest edge of the archipelago and 26 kilometres (160 miles) north of Malé, with around 16 inhabited islands and a population of some 9,000. Its capital is on Diddu. Utheemu was the birthplace of Sultan Mohamed Thakurufaanu, the vanquisher of the Portuguese in 1573; it has a small museum. Kela was a British base during the Second World War, the northern counterpart of Gan. Turukunu is the most northern island of all, and is noted for its pretty girls and dancing.

## South Thiladhunmathi—B

The capital is Nolivaranfaru, though the most populous island is Kuluduffushi, most of whose workers have already migrated to Malé, leaving only some 12,000 in the atoll, which is served by one of the Maldives' two regional hospitals. It also boasts the highest island in the archipelago, Faridu, elevation 6 metres (20 feet), and principally famous for its toddy. Lots of wreck dives, especially near Mukunudu, which also has some of the best fishing grounds.

## North Miladhunmadulu—C

Just under 200 kilometres (124 miles) from Malé, with 15 inhabited islands and a population of around 7,000. The capital, Faru Kolu Funadu, has a good harbour and the ruins of an ancient mosque, and 700-year-old tombstones. The atoll is famed for the turtles that breed on its beaches.

## South Miladhunmadulu—D

Numbering 14 inhabited islands amongst almost 60 that aren't, and with a total population of around 6,500. Velidhu and Holudu are the most populous islands though Munadu is the capital. A 40-foot ruin on Landu appears to be a relic left by Thor Heyerdahl's mysterious ancient traveller, the *Redin*.

## North Maalhosmadulu—E
Sixteen peopled islands and 65 uninhabited ones make up this atoll, whose capital is Ungoofaru. A total of 9,000 people live here and Kandoludu even suffers the same problem as Malé, overpopulation. It has the best fishing in the whole archipelago, especially near Alifushi, an island famous for its skilled boatmakers and site of the main government boat yard supplying *dhonis* throughout the country. Renowned craftsmen also live on Inguraidu and Innamaadu.

## South Maalhosmadulu—F
Thirteen inhabited islands and more than 50 that are not, with a population of about 7,000. The best fishing grounds are near Eyadafushi, Hitadu, and Tuladu. *Feyli* weaving (for women's sarongs) and lacquerwork boxes are manufactured on Tulusdhu and Fehendu islands. Fuludu was the site of the shipwreck of the *Corbin*, which kept François Pyrard de Laval in the Maldives. It was also the place of banishment of a German tourist who murdered his girlfriend in the mid-70s. Goidu and Fehendu are also prison islands.

## Faadhippolhu—G
Just 120 kilometres (75 miles) from Malé, Faadhippolhu comprises four inhabited islands with the capital on Naifaru. The fishing is good, second only to South Maalnosmadulu. Handicrafts include mother-of-pearl and black coral.

## Malé —H
Includes North and South Malé Atolls and the smaller Gaafaru; the atoll office is on Thulusdhu. Outside of the almost 40 resorts, and the nation's capital, only nine islands are inhabited with a population of around 9,000, mainly on Kashidhu in the far north and Guraidhoo in the south. The best fishing is reputedly near Dhiffushi.

## Ari—I
Includes Rasdhu and Toddu, two tiny atolls north of Ari, the main atoll. The capital is Mahibadu on the eastern side of the atoll, which has a total population of nearly 8,000. The coral used in Malé is quarried mainly from Fenfushi and Maamigili in the south. Toddu is famed for its watermelons.

## Felidhu—J
The most sparsely inhabited atoll of them all, with only 1,500 people on five islands—and obviously destined to become a big tourist area. It has great diving sites like Shark Point, and an unspoilt fishing village at Mundu.

# The Atolls of Maldives

N

North Thiladhanmathi Atoll

South Thiladhanmathi Atoll

| 0 | 25 | 50 | 75 km |

| 0 | 25 | 50 miles |

Makunudu

Reef

North Miladhumadulu Atoll

Alifushi

South Miladhumadulu Atoll

North Maalhosmadulu Atoll

Faadhippolhu Atoll

South Maalhosmadulu Atoll

Kashidu

Gaarfaru

Goidu

North Malé Atoll

Teddu

Rasdu

Indian

MALE

Ari Atoll

South Male Atoll

Ocean

Felidhu Atoll

North Nilandhe Atoll

Mulaku Atoll

South Nilandhe Atoll

Kolhumadulu Atoll

Hadhdhunmathi Atoll

Indian

Reef

Ocean

North Huvadu Atoll

South Huvado Atoll

Equator

Faammulaku Atoll

Addu Atoll

1000 m

## Mulaku—K

Nine islands with about 3,000 people. The capital is Muli, although the biggest island is Dhiggaru. No agriculture at all in this atoll.

## North Nilandhe—L

This tiny atoll has only five inhabited islands and just 2,000 souls. Heyerdahl raved about the wonders of the capital, Nilandhu, which seem to be more conjectural than based on actual evidence. The fishing is not so good but it is famous for the turtles that beach on Darabudu during the southwest monsoon period between April and October.

## South Nilandhe—M

Eight inhabited islands 150 kilometres (93 miles) south of Malé. The capital, Kudahuvadu, another site praised by Heyerdahl, has a mosque with the finest fingerprint masonry anywhere in the world. The population of 3,000 includes skilled goldsmiths on Rimbadu and Huludeli.

## Kolhumadulu—N

One of the very best atolls for fishing, especially near Villifushi, Guraidu and Timarafushi. The capital is Veymandu, and the total population of about 7,000 are spread over 13 islands. More than 50 others are uninhabited.

## Hadhdhunmathi—O

The atoll that has it all—good fishing, extensive Buddhist remains, and over 1,000 acres under cultivation. Twelve populated islands with 7,000 people, 75 other islands empty. The capital is Hitadu, though Gamu is bigger. Relics include the mystery dome at Isdu. There's a small airfield on Kadhu.

## North Huvadu—P

The first atoll south of the 60-mile-wide One and Half Degree Channel. Ten inhabited islands amongst 83 empty ones. The capital is Villingili, population 500.

## South Huvadu—Q

This atoll, 340 kilometres (211 miles) south of Malé, has 154 empty islands and only ten populated ones, though with 9,000 inhabitants. Strangely, the usual Maldivian gender balance is reversed here, with women outnumbering men. The biggest island is Tinadu which has very good fishing, its own dialect—very different from northern speech—and a history of separatism that saw it burnt down during the last big revolt in 1962, after which it was empty for four years. Gaddu and Fiyori produce beautiful *tundu kuna* mats using local reeds.

## Foammulaku—R

A single-island atoll, population 4,000, with the best soil in the Maldives, and two freshwater lakes. Taro is cultivated here in special pits, and mangoes. On the other hand, it has a treacherous reef, an angry sea and poor fishing. However, the people look bigger and healthier than elsewhere; it must be the fruit. There is no safe anchorage, but the island attracts visitors thanks to the aeroplane connection with Addu.

## Addu—S

The southernmost atoll in the Maldives and almost 500 kilometres (310 miles) from Malé, Addu has a very well protected harbour lagoon only accessible through four entrances, and is surrounded by barrier reefs. The population is high, around 14,000. The fishing is no good and atoll life is dominated by the old RAF base on Gan, that now has two garment factories and a government-run guesthouse at which no sensible tourist would wish to stay. The old Koagannu cemetery on Meedu is said to be historically significant.

# Resorts

The price ranges of resorts are for a double room in peak season.

## North Malé Atoll

### US$220 +

■ KUDAHITHI

An élite adjunct to Boduhithi—boat crossings are free of charge—this eight-year-old resort is supposed to be one of the most exclusive retreats in the Maldives with its six luxurious 'theme' bungalows and just 12 beds. Although well-maintained, it feels a bit self-consciously isolated and certainly does not compare with Cocoa Island, which charges comparable rates. It is also very, very small.

Popular with business people, it is usually fully booked in peak season. Eighteen staff lurk discreetly to attend to your needs and serve the food produced by an Italian-trained local chef. Activities and amenities are shared with Boduhithi. The 'Arabian Room' comes with a video, a bathroom done out in Italian marble and a bath shaped like a giant plastic clam with brass fittings. The 'Maharani Room' has Indian furniture. Other rooms illustrate a nautical theme with ships' maps and fittings, and a safari room has leopard skin tiles, a plastic crocodile and fake zebra-striped bedspread. The 'Maldivian Room' is the nicest with a bed carved in the shape of a *dhoni*, and a traditional well and open-air toilet in the leafy garden.

Transfer:  29 kilometres (18 miles) from the airport, three hours by *dhoni* or one hour by speedboat, $50.

Booking:  Safari Tours, 1 Chandhani Magu, Malé: Tel. 32–3524, 3760; fax. 32–2516; tlx. 66030 SAFARI MF. Resort: Tel. & fax. 44–4613.

■ MAKUNUDHU

The name means 'pestilence island' in Dhivehi, something which makes the local fishermen chuckle, for the name is at odds with the resort's delightful aspect and its wide and clear lagoon. Swiss-run and very exclusive, Makunudhu caters mainly to stressed-out, security-conscious Europeans in search of soporific luxury. This small, beautiful, sheltered island hides 31 rooms, with IDD telephone and a personal safe deposit. However, there is no airconditioning on the island. The chef serves delicate dishes *à la nouvelle cuisine*, and among the boutiques there's even room for a beautician. Well-equipped diving school, wide range of watersports amenities, and a good anchorage for passing yachts.

Transfer:   34 kilometres (21 miles) from the airport, $75 by speedboat.
Booking:    Gelina Maldives, 7 Orchid Magu, Malé: Tel. 32–4742; fax. 32–4465;
            tlx. 77068 GAL MF. Resort: Tel. 44–6464; fax. 44–6565; tlx. 77059
            MAKU MF.

## ■ VABBINFARU

This is an exceptionally beautiful island. It was one of the original five resorts which
launched the Maldives as a tourist destination in the early 1970s. The resort, staffed
by ten Europeans and forty Maldivians, is very popular with Swiss and Belgians. The
emphasis is suitably gastronomic; the French chef even makes fresh croissants,
pastries and bread in the island's bakery. The main restaurant has a tall roof and is
open to the elements atrium-style, so that sun, sand and sea blend together. The set
menus for lunch and dinner are excellent.

Vabbinfaru is quite small with only 30 bungalows set back from lovely sandy
avenues of coconut palms, 'magoo' and bougainvillea shrubs. Two bungalows lie near
the sea, the waves lapping at the front door on a tiny private beach; these are for
families, the split-level rooms housing three or four beds. The other cottages are
thatched, circular, airy A-frames, built using natural screw pine matting, *satta* mats
and *kunnar* rattan—a simple decor with a pleasant and natural feel emphasized by
the whitewashed coral walls and the spacious, tiled bathrooms. The resort shop is
well-stocked with fashionable clothes made by Barbara Sansoni, a Shri Lankan
designer, with lovely jewellery and scarves. Very elegant and continental. The aviary
adds to the air of refinement.

The beach is perfect for swimming and snorkelling, a gentle smooth lagoon with
a fine sand bottom is protected by the house reef about 50 metres (165 feet) out.
There is a fully equipped diving school. Other activities range from catamaran sailing
to fishing, windsurfing, and mini tennis. A speedboat is available for hire.
Transfer:   Half an hour by speedboat.
Booking:    Dhiram, Faamudheyri Magu, Malé: Tel. 32–3369.
            Resort: Tel. 44–3147; fax. 44–3843; tlx. 77026 VABBIN MF.

# US$150–220

## ■ BODUHITHI

A decade old, Boduhithi has recently been renovated at a cost of $3.5 million as the
new Club Vacanze jet-set destination and looks every bit as good as the brochures
hint it should be. The 87 thatched bungalows have spacious and elegant rooms,
furnished with Malaysian and Thai artwork. Some overlook the sea on stilts. Black-
tiled bathrooms are finished in wood, the design similiar to the up-market Gangehi
resort which used the same architect. Boasts a theatre area, disco and Maldivian
restaurant. One of the best all-round deals in the archipelago.

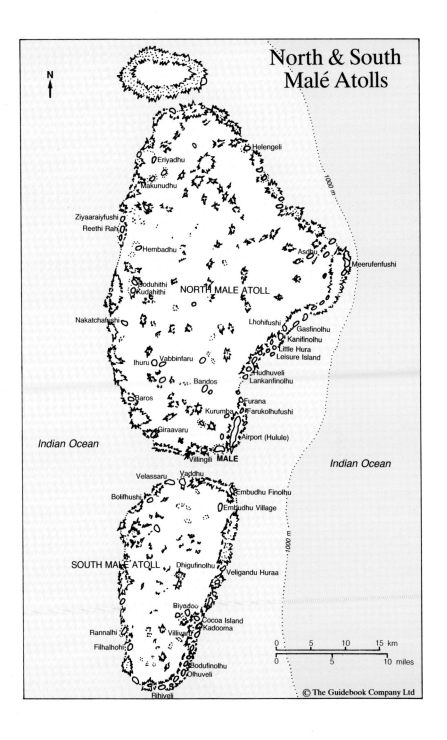

# North & South Malé Atolls

N

Helengeli

Eriyadhu

Makunudhu

Ziyaaraiyfushi
Reethi Rah

Hembadhu

Asdhu

Meerufenfushi

Boduhithi
Kudahithi

NORTH MALE ATOLL

Nakatchafushi

Lhohifushi

Gasfinolhu

Kanifinolhu

Little Hura
Leisure Island

Ihuru

Vabbinfaru

Bandos

Hudhuveli
Lankanfinolhu

Baros

Furana

Kurumba

Farukolhufushi

Giraavaru

Airport (Hulule)

Indian Ocean

Villingili   **MALE**

Velassaru

Vaddhu

Bolifhushi

Embudhu Finolhu

Embudhu Village

Indian Ocean

SOUTH MALE ATOLL

Dhigufinolhu

Veligandu Huraa

Biyadoo

Cocoa Island

Rannalhi

Villivaru

Kadooma

Filhalhohi

Bodufinolhu

Olhuveli

Rihiveli

1000 m

1000 m

0        5        10        15 km

0            5            10 miles

© The Guidebook Company Ltd

Transfer:   29 kilometres (18 miles) from the airport, 3 hours by *dhoni*, 45 minutes by speedboat, $50 one-way.

Booking:   Safari Tours, 1 Chandhani Magu, Malé: Tel. 32–3524, 3760; fax. 32–2516; tlx. 66030 SAFARI MF. Resort: Tel. 44–5905; fax. 44–2634; tlx. 77044 BODHITI MF.

### ■ CLUB MED FARUKOLHUFUSHI

From a distance, Club Med looks like a cluster of *dhoni* sails emerging from the palm trees; close-up, the distinctive architecture appears rather frayed around the edges and in need of an overhaul. Despite Club Med's 'swinging singles' reputation, the unattached are not really encouraged to come here; the management prefers to highlight family entertainment. A lot of money has been spent on renovation—$6 million back in 1985—but the atmosphere remains rather tacky and geared towards package groups. The second largest resort in the Maldives, Club Med does not allow day-visitors or occasional overnight stays. Its 55 European staff rotate every six months, in stark contrast to smaller, family-run resorts. The Japanese like it because of its 'theme' approach.

The 152 triple, non-airconditioned rooms are grouped into 19 blocks of apartments; the design is functional and spartan. Buffet meals are served in a large cabana-style, open-air hangar and feature Japanese, Italian, Maldivian, and other Asian dishes.

The main attraction for many is the resort's diving school, which with nine instructors is the largest in the Maldives (known disdainfully in other resorts as a 'diving factory'). Beginners' courses run daily for four to five days. They are all CMAS, not PADI or NAUI, and are well organized. There are about ten good diving spots within an hour's boat ride; group excursions are kept to a maximum of six divers. The school insists on a compulsory medical check-up and has good emergency facilities, including a resident diving doctor. The decompression chamber here is one of four in the Maldives. Video recording equipment is available for hire.

The resort operates the 'bead money' system used by Club Med worldwide. There is an efficient reservation and transport office; nightclub and bar with set meals; boutique and crafts centre. Pleasure trips are available to Thulagiri, Himafushi, and Malé, with round trip prices $26 (adult), $13 (child). Other activities include snorkelling (courses available), picnics, aerobics, yoga, a water gym, Club Med tournaments, sailing and windsurfing (the large, shallow reef is good for windsurfing).

Transfer:   Two kilometres (one mile) from the airport, about 15 minutes by *dhoni*, $10 one-way.

Booking:    1 Ibrahim Hassan Didi Magu, Majeedee Baazaar, Malé: Tel. 32–2976;
            fax. 32–2850. Resort: Tel. 44–4552; fax. 44–2415; tlx. 66057
            MEDMALD MF.

■ FURANA—FULL MOON ISLAND
An upmarket resort with white sandy beaches and a large lagoon. The 156 rooms are
airconditioned, with bath, shower, telephone, music, hairdryer and minibar, and are
decorated to a high standard. In addition, to the main restaurant and coffee shop,
there are Thai and Chinese restaurants and beach barbecues. Facilities include a
disco, shop, gymnasium and tennis court, with excursions, diving and windsurfing
amongst the leisure activities.
Transfer:   20 minutes from the airport.
Booking:    Universal Enterprises, 38 Orchid Magu, Malé: Tel. 32–2971;
            fax. 32–2678; tlx. 66024 UNIENT MF.

■ GASFINOLHU
Small-scale resort of 60 beds in 20 cabana-style huts, ten-year-old Gasfinolhu aims to
be an exclusive resort. Its name translates as 'tree on a sandbank'. All double rooms
include bathrooms with hot and cold water. Diving, snorkelling, canoeing,
windsurfing, beach volleyball and ping pong are available. Discos and the occasional
evening shows are also organised.
Transfer:   20 kilometres (13 miles) from the airport.
Booking:    Dhirham Travels and Chandling, Malé: Tel. 32–3371; fax. 32–4752;
            tlx. 66027. Resort: Tel. 44–2078; fax 44–5941; tlx. 77050.

■ GIRAAVARU
This resort has 50 luxury, appointed, airconditioned rooms, all with piped music, hot
and cold water, hair dryers, minibar and IDD facilities. A tastefully designed public
area blended with Maldivian architecture consists of two well-stocked bars. There is
also a poolside restaurant with banquetting facilities, and floodlit volleyball, a tennis
court, freshwater swimming pool, disco, coffee shop and a selection of small shops,
not to mention the super diving to be had on the Vadhoo channel. The food here is
some of the best in the archipelago. Though the resort is only 15 minutes from Malé
by speedboat, it nonetheless offers total seclusion.
Transfer:   11 kilometres (seven miles) from the airport, $30 by *dhoni*.
Booking:    Phoenix Hotels & Resorts, Fasmeeru, Marine Drive, Malé:
            Tel. 32–3181, 3587; fax. 32–5499; tlx. 66107 HORIZON MF. Resort:
            Tel. 44–0440; fax. 44–4818; tlx. 66059 GIRAVAR MF.

■ IHURU

Oval-shaped Ihuru has a bed capacity of 88, with rooms in semi-detached bungalows. The resort has a restaurant, bar and coffee shop. It is said to be the most photographed island in the Maldives and is often used as a backdrop for commercials because its scenery captures the essence of Maldivian perfection and isolation. The house reef, known as 'The Wall', is a particularly spectacular diving spot. Activities include windsurfing, catamaran sailing, canoeing, scuba diving, table tennis, volleyball, badminton, night-fishing, island hopping and excursions to Malé.

*A favourite past-time, smoking a hookah*

Transfer: 16 kilometres (ten miles) from the airport, $30 by *dhoni*.
Booking: Ihuru Investments, H Bodukosheege, Ameeru Ahmed Magu, Malé: Tel. 32–6720; fax. 32–6700. Resort: Tel. 44–3502; fax. 44–5933; tlx. 66099.

■ KANIFINOLHU

Kanifinolhi is just under one kilometre (half a mile) long and 178 metres (196 yards) wide. Its plentiful vegetation makes it one of the more physically attractive resorts, and its white sandy beaches and the extended lagoon make it perfect for water sports at any time of the year. The island is fringed by a beautiful reef where snorkelling reveals an endless variety of fish, especially at the northern end. Boat trips to the reef run every morning and afternoon.

The resort combines traditional with modern architecture and is quite spartan. It is popular with younger visitors, especially Swedes, Japanese, and those from Hong Kong. Visitors tend to rate it for the atmosphere, which is young and fun. There are 13 bungalows served by 130 staff including 13 foreigners. The 130 rooms are very modern—high ceilings and nicely landscaped, giving a fresh and modern feel. Hot and cold desalinated water is on tap; all rooms have refrigerators, and the deluxe ones are airconditioned. The good facilities available include boat rental, bank, post office, disco, shops and a travel agency. The restaurant serves Asian and western food.

Club EuroDivers operates the diving school with four instructors, who offer all PADI courses up to Divemaster. Other facilities include Hobie-cats, parasailing, windsurfing, water-skiing, tennis, table tennis, badminton and billiards. Excellent snorkelling from *dhoni*s with a free boat to the reef twice a day.

Transfer: 19 kilometres (12 miles) from the airport, $25 return by *dhoni*.

Booking: Cyprea Hotels & Travel, 25 Marine Drive, Malé: Tel. 32–5367, 2451; fax. 32–3523; tlx. 66026 CYPREA MF. Resort: Tel. 44–3152; fax. 44–4859; tlx. 77096 EUROKAN MF.

### ■ KURUMBA

If you asked an hotel architect to design a resort hotel in paradise this is exactly what he or she might have created: a top-class establishment that still seems just like an international hotel transported to an otherwise deserted island, right down to the drinks in each room's minibar.

Kurumba is just three kilometres (1.9 miles) from the

*Viewing the world from a different perspective*

airport, or ten minutes by speedboat. This was the very first resort to open back in 1972. US$15 million has been spent since then renovating its plush cabana-style architecture and extensive facilities. The one kilometre-long (half-mile) island is attractively landscaped; clumps of bougainvillea, frangipani shrubs and palm trees ensure privacy between individual cottage units. All 156 twin rooms and eight double-storeyed suites are airconditioned, furnished with imported materials from Singapore, and with fresh flowers daily on the dressing tables. Lots of natural wood and Maldivian-style pillars create a very natural effect, countered by wall-to-wall carpeting and piped-in music. Connecting rooms and duplexes are available for families.

Facilities are on a grand scale after a massive upgrade in 1987. Adjacent large, A-frame buildings house a restaurant, shopping complex, and a conference centre with capacity for 500. The two main restaurants serve Chinese and north Indian food; a 24-hour coffee shop completes the hotel atmosphere. The food selection is suitably broad, accented on fresh seafood. The *all'aperto* dining area on the sand turns into a seafood barbecue at night. Food is flown in thrice weekly from Japan and New Zealand, and is correspondingly high-priced. The bar, nestling under a huge *dhoni*-shaped A-frame and outfitted with nautical furnishings, is one of the best-stocked in the archipelago. Close to Malé, Kurumba attracts day-and-evening trippers, and offers live entertainment in its strobe-lit, open-air, nightly disco.

There is a large fleet of speedboats for pleasure trips, glass-bottomed boats to tour the reef, day or night-fishing for garoupa and red snapper, plus the range of sailing, windsurfing, and scuba facilities. The large diving school run by EuroDivers of Switzerland is well rated by the expatriate community in Malé. Uniquely, Kurumba possesses an excellent sports gym complete with jacuzzi, three floodlit tennis courts, a freshwater swimming pool, and an airconditioned billiards room.

Transfer:   A fifteen-minute *dhoni*-ride from Malé or the airport, for $10.

Booking:   Universal Enterprises, 38 Orchid Magu, Malé: Tel. 32–3080/2971/3 512; fax. 32–2678; tlx. 66024 UNIENT MF. Resort: Tel. 44–3081; fax. 44–3885; tlx. 77083 KURUMBA MF.

■ THULAGIRI

The resort is a small coral island with tropical vegetation surrounded by crystal clear lagoons, with thousands of colourful fish housed in a magnificent coral garden. It is only a ten-minute stroll to encompass the whole island. Facilities include IDD telephone, telex, telefax, a restaurant with an international buffet, coffee shop, bar and freshwater swimming pool. All 55 deluxe rooms are air-conditioned, and have minibars and en suite bathrooms with hot and cold water. Sports facilities include volleyball, badminton, diving, windsurfing, catamaran sailing, jet skiing, water-skiing, darts, carom and table tennis.

Transfer:    11 kilometres (seven miles) from the airport, about 45 minutes by *dhoni*, $23 from Club Med.

Booking:    H Jareeza, 15 Marine Drive, Malé: Tel. 32–2844; fax. 32–1026; tlx. 77061 ORCHID MF. Resort: Tel. 44–5929; fax. 44–5939; tlx. 77110.

# US$80–150

## ■ ASDHU

A tiny, idyllic island run by Maldivian entrepreneur, Ahmed Ismail, who also runs the Nasandhura Palace Hotel in Malé. Asdhu is refreshingly simple with an unpretentious style yet high-quality management, and is very popular with Italians who appreciate its intimacy, small-scale charms and excellent diving school. The 60-bed resort is run as a tight ship. The staff are all Maldivian, apart from a Shri Lankan cook, and they all double up on activities and jobs. There are 30 whitewashed cottages, all immaculately kept and very private with slatted wooden shutters and parquet floors. One lovely Maldivian feature is the woven coir net blinds which open to the sea and sky so you can hear the sound of the waves. Good selection of wines, cocktails and food in the restaurant.

The diving school has three instructors and keeps its teacher/pupil ratio as low as one to three. The chief instructor, Fabio Valenti, has been in Asdhu for four years and has mapped out 27 dive sites within a half-hour *dhoni*-ride, including one place where you can watch sleeping whitetip sharks. PADI courses are offered in German, Italian and English. Also windsurfing and night-diving, and excursions to the fishing village on Dhiffushi.

Transfer:    43 kilometres (27 miles) from the airport, $30 by *dhoni*.

Booking:    C/o Shoanary, Henveiru, Malé: Tel. 32–2149; fax. 32–4300; tlx. 66091 POLYCOM MF. Resort: Tel. 44–5051.

## ■ BANDOS

Bandos used to be famous for its shark-feeding antics—expert divers would allow a shark to approach and eat fish from their hands and mouth—but this practice is now discouraged for fear of subverting the sharks' docility. Bandos has increased its capacity to 400 beds which is very large by Maldivian standards. It's also used by many airlines as their stopover hotel.

The renovations have made a huge difference to the island's facilities. The Health Club houses a steam bath and a freshwater swimming pool. A sports complex offers badminton, squash, jacuzzi, gymnasium and aerobics. Baby-sitting services cater for the family visitor, IDD and fax for the compulsive communicator.

Of the 125-plus airconditioned rooms, 40 are suites. The rooms are grouped in blocks, some newer, a larger number somewhat spartan, but all the same price. A set-menu main restaurant vies with an alternative serving Chinese food, a 24-hour coffee shop serving Asian and European dishes, and 24-hour room service. There is live music in the Sand Bar—ersatz Maldivian calypso and troupes performing the *bodu beru* dance on 'Maldivian Nights'. A leisure centre offers squash, sauna and beauty salon.

Outdoor recreation facilities include catamaran sailing. The diving school offers PADI and NAUI courses; a week's unlimited diving from a boat, exclusive of equipment hire; and a standard dive with full equipment. Excursions to the nearby uninhabited island of Kuda Bandos can be made for snorkelling and picnics.

Transfer:   Eight kilometres (five miles) from the airport, about ten minutes by speedboat, $20 return.

Booking:   Bandos Malé Office, H Jazeera, Marine Drive, Malé: Tel. 32–2844; fax. 32–1026; tlx. 77061 ORCHID MF. Resort: Tel. 44–0088; fax. 44–3877; tlx. 66050 BANDOS MF.

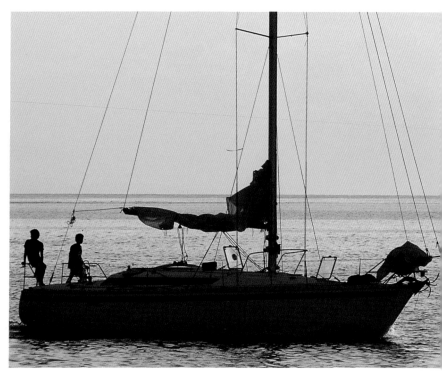

*Taking life easy on the open sea*

■ BAROS

Well-established (it has been operating since 1973) Baros, the 'half-moon shaped island', is popular with German and British package tourists. Its 50 recently renovated rooms stand in ten rows of four, facing the sea. Rooms are airconditioned. The renovation added a new coffee shop and beach barbecue. The main restaurant is thatched with a mini fountain in an *all'aperto* arrangement; live music once a week. The bar opposite is furnished in a nautical style with a boutique. A welcome drink and cool towel is given on arrival.

Excursions to other islands, night-fishing, buffet evenings and trips to Malé are offered. The well-equipped diving club is run by the Munich-based Sub-Aqua Reisen. PADI diving courses stress careful adjustment to the waters, eleven dives here instead of eight as in most resorts to qualify for the Open Water certificate, in small classes of four. Catamaran hire, windsurfing and water-skiing are also available.

Transfer:    Eight kilometres (five miles) from the airport, $20 return by *dhoni*.

Booking:    Universal Enterprises, 38 Orchid Magu, Malé: Tel. 32–3080, 2971, 3512; fax. 32–2678; tlx 66024 UNIENT MF. Resort: Tel. 44–2672; fax. 44–3497.

■ ERIYADHU

This resort has 92 beds in 45 bungalows by the water's edge, each with freshwater showers. The rooms are fan-cooled. Eriyadhu is one of the cheaper resorts because of its distance from civilization, but is blessed with a good house reef, a wide beach and a fine lagoon. Diving is organized by the Swiss Sub-Aqua Club. Live music, discos and Maldivian folk dances are amongst the evening entertainments.

Transfer:    39 kilometres (24 miles) from the airport, almost three hours and $35 by *dhoni*.

Booking:    AAA Trading Company, Ibrahim Hassan Didi Magu, Malé: Tel. 32–2417; fax. 32–5926; tlx. 66031 ERIYADU MF. Resort: Tel. 44–4487; fax. 44–4943.

■ HEMBADHU

Forty-six beach-fronted bungalows with attached bathrooms mark this small and remote resort. The rooms range from standard to deluxe, and most of the rooms are airconditioned and have minibars. This resort is popular with German groups looking for something a little remote and exclusive. It is carefully looked after and unpretentious. Facilities include a restaurant, bar, souvenir shop, diving school and water sports centre with windsurfing, water-skiing, parasailing and catamaran sailing. Other activities include volleyball and table tennis.

Transfer:    39 kilometres (24 miles) from the airport, $30 by *dhoni*.

Booking:    Transit Inn, Maaveyo Magu, Malé: Tel. 32–2016; fax. 32–6606.
            Resort: Tel. 44–3884; fax. 44–1948; tlx. 66084 JEWORLD MF.

■ HUDHUVELI

Adjacent to Bandos, Hudhuveli is run by the same agency in Malé. Named after its beautiful stretch of white sand, this is a much quieter resort with simple beachcombing-style accomodation, ideal for honeymooners. There are 44 thatched and rather spartan cottages, though they do have fresh water in the rooms and 24-hour room service. The resort appeals mainly to British and German tourists. This is a good island for young people and children, being not too far from Malé and with a safe lagoon. The diving school is run by two Austrians, and is highly rated by the Italian cruise yacht skippers, diving instructors, and expatriates in Malé. Windsurfing conditions are ideal inside the large lagoon and a free boat goes to the outer reef twice a day for snorkelling. The bar has an adjoining disco in the evenings. It is said to be possible to make visits to Himmafushi fishing village.

Transfer:   14 kilometres (nine miles) from the airport, about 50 minutes by
            *dhoni*, $20
Booking:    Deens Orchid Agency, H Jareeza, Marine Drive, Malé: Tel. 32–3779,
            2844; fax. 32–1026; tlx. 77061 ORCHID MF. Resort: Tel. 44–3396,
            3982-3; fax. 44–3849; tlx. 77035 HUDVELI MF.

■ LHOHIFUSHI

Opened a decade ago in the vanguard of the tourist boom, Lhohifushi appeals mainly to German, English and Swiss package tourists in search of an economical paradise. The 60 basic, thatched huts are simply furnished in local materials with ceiling fans. The island has a laid-back, slightly hippie atmosphere right down to the hammocks in the trees. It has recently been upgraded to include a Chinese restaurant, two coffee shops, and freshwater supplies from two desalinization plants.

The diving school offers PADI courses up to Advanced Open Water and Rescue Standard. Good coral reef for snorkelling and diving. Weekly excursions to Meerufenfushi, Asdu, Tulusdu and the fishing village at Dhiffushi.

Transfer:   17 kilometres (11 miles) from the airport.
Booking:    Altaf Enterprises, Ibrahim Hassan Didi Magu, Malé: Tel. 32–3378;
            fax 32–4783; tlx 66047 ALTAF MF. Resort: Tel. 44–1909;
            fax 44–1908.

■ LITTLE HURA

A lower to mid-range resort, Little Hura's 43 cottages are grouped in the middle of the island so that visitors have a choice between the two beaches on opposite sides.

Visitors to Little Hura rate its friendly atmosphere as one of the main attractions. There is a fully equipped diving school, a water sports centre which provides water skiing, windsurfing, canoes, catamaran sailing and parasailing. There are also island hopping trips, excursions to Malé and night fishing. One nice touch is the short walk across tidal sands that leads you to a deserted islet, confusingly called Hura.

Transfer:   16 kilometres (ten miles) from the airport, $20 (by *dhonis*).

Booking:   Hotel Alia, Haveeree Higun, Malé: Tel. 32–2197; tlx. 77032 HOTALIA MF. Resort: Tel. 44–5934; fax. 44–4231.

### ■ NAKATCHAFUSHI

A perfect, teardrop-shaped island with many varieties of colourful birds and insects. The shallow, sandy lagoon and long strip of sand washed clean by the sea make this island especially suitable for families with small children. Nakatchafushi attracts many people who return again and again, mainly British and Germans. Accommodation is in 60 immaculate units, most of which are round with thatched roofs. This pleasantly landscaped 'honeymooners' retreat' has a nice feel with its whitewashed walls and natural furnishings. All rooms are airconditioned and the *en suite* bathrooms have hot and cold desalinated water.

An open-sided restaurant and a coffee shop that spills out onto the sands provide perfectly adequate food, while drinks can be enjoyed at the terraced bar on a pleasant wooden deck jutting into the lagoon; the bar also doubles as a disco. The food is mainly continental with specialist buffets and barbecues. Breakfast is the culinary highlight. A Chinese restaurant has just been added. A welcome drink and cool towel on arrival is a pleasing touch.

The surrounding waters have plenty of coral and fish. Night-fishing and big-game fishing can be arranged. Sports include diving, catamaran sailing, windsurfing, parasailing, water-skiing, snorkelling, canoeing, volleyball, and table tennis. The resort's two diving instructors, Hans and Christine Hohensinn-Zedelmayer, have lived here for six years and run the Barrakuda International diving school with a local Maldivian divemaster. They offer eight-lesson CMAS and eleven-lesson PADI Open Water courses, spread over four or six days starting twice a week. Around 500–600 people take these courses every year. A fleet of boats is available for relaxing excursions to other islands, including Hemadhu and Rasfari just half an hour away. IDD and fax facilities are available at reception.

Transfer :   23 kilometres (14 miles) from the airport, $30 by *dhoni*.

Booking:   Universal Enterprises, 38 Orchid Magu, Malé: Tel. 32–3080, 2971, 3512; fax. 32–2678; tlx. 66024 UNIENT MF. Resort: Tel. 44–3846/7; fax. 44–2665.

*(following pages) Sports Day celebrations at the National Stadium, Malé*

## The Greenhouse Effect

Climatic cycles and change are a normal feature of the earth's atmosphere, but over the last two centuries natural change has been overshadowed by man-made change. The increased burning of fossil fuels and release of carbon dioxide into the air is altering the make-up of the atmosphere and raising its temperature. The United Nations Intergovernmental Panel on Climate Change reported recently that if nothing is done to change the way we live, by the end of the next century the world could be 2.5° C (4.5°F) warmer and the sea level 0.75 metres (2.5 feet) higher, differences that could signify the Maldives becoming the first civilization since Atlantis to simply disappear beneath the waves.

There are several reasons why this prediction may not come true, and a few good ones why the Maldivians are worried that it will. The sea level may rise because of the melting of the polar ice-caps and the thermal expansion of the oceans as they heat up, both changes that would follow the actual warming of the atmosphere. The main problem for the coral reefs of the Maldives would be that the water temperature could rise too high for the corals to survive.

Coral can live in seawater temperatures of 16–36°C (61–97°F) but for optimum growth the range is 23–25°C (73–77°F). Average annual water temperatures in the Maldives are 25–29°C (77–84°F), so the waters here are already around the upper limit for active reef-building. If sea temperatures were to increase very gradually, no doubt the corals could evolve and adapt to cope with the change. But any sudden rise in temperature (and an average increase of even 1°C over 100 years is quite dramatic in evolutionary terms) could be bad news for the Maldivian reefs.

Other climatic changes could also effect the reefs' survival. Increased cloud cover and rainfall might decrease the ability of the symbiotic algae within the coral to photosynthesize food and oxygen, which in turn would effect the rate of growth of the reef. And the Indian Ocean already has a low concentration of dissolved oxygen. Furthermore, it is losing more water by evaporation than is replenished by rain, so is gradually becoming more saline. The salinity level, like temperature, is quite critical for coral growth and only a narrow range can be tolerated.

The whole question of climatic change is actually very complex, and the possible effects are hard to predict. To make matters even more complicated, not all scientists are convinced that the world is facing a catastrophic global warming. They are in a minority, but their arguments are well-reasoned and sincerely held.

One problem that the Maldives may face—coastal flooding—is not necessarily caused by long-term variation of the sea-level but the combination of high tides, storms and wave action. Three tidal waves in 18 months in the mid-1980s forced many islanders to leave their homes and turned Malé into a temporary lake. In a country where the average altitude is 1.5 metres (five feet) above sea level, building defences is going to be important. Natural reef defences will have to be strengthened, water and food supplies diversified, and building standards adapted. Waves in the Maldives are generally light—three-metre (ten feet) swells are exceptional—so storm defences are not well established. What is more, long narrow islands are the least amenable to engineering protection, which is a last resort anyway. As President Gayoom put it at the Small States Conference on Sea Level Rise in Malé, in November 1989, 'no realistic solutions to our problems have yet been identified' adding that he did not want Maldivians to become environmental refugees.

One area of uncertainty concerns the sea level itself. The net trend in the Pacific and Indian Oceans over the last 3,000 years has been a slight fall in sea level, a fact borne out by several studies over the last 50 years. The sea level today is close to its level during the last interglacial period, about one metre (3.3 feet) higher than during an Ice Age when water is incorporated into the polar ice sheets. Indeed, the last interglacial, 120,000 years ago, may have been slightly warmer than now with a higher sea level. The latest predictions suggest a 3.7–5.8 millimetre (0.14–0.23 inches) annual rise with guesstimates of around 30–40 centimetres (11.8–15.7 inches) by the year 2050; many estimates are higher, some lower. Underlying this is the fact that no one is sure exactly how reef islands are actually built, or what their growth rates are. There is some evidence from islands in the Pacific that coral can catch up after a period of glaciation and subsequent sea level rise. For now it looks a safe bet though to say that although the next 50 years may be OK, the world could be facing more serious problems in a century from now.

■ REETHI RAH

This Swiss-run resort of 100 beds is secluded and chic, fully living up to its local name of Medhufinolhu, 'the beautiful island'. The setting is simply superb, with a protective reef on the leeward side enclosing a broad, shallow lagoon of glass-smooth translucent water, perfect for learning to dive or windsurf. The 50 palm-thatched, whitewashed coral bunglows blend harmoniously with the lush vegetation and well-raked white sand, and are strung along the eastern beach facing the sea linked by a single path.

Interiors of the individual units are simple, meticulously clean, and aesthetically pleasing with plenty of natural wood and coir matting. Ventilation is provided by an ingenious woven screen that leaves the room partially open to the sky, a nice Maldivian touch. Reethi Rah attracts mainly Swiss and German executive types who return year after year. It discourages package tours to protect its intimacy. The kitchen can fulfill most breakfast requests, from pancakes to delicious fluffy omelettes, and serves an excellent espresso. Lavish buffets of Maldivian food, mainly curries and grilled fish, complement continental menus. The main restaurant has a billowy canvas roof with prettily laid-out tables on a floor of soft sand next to the well-stocked bar. Tucked away elsewhere on the island, another hideaway bar hovers over the water on stilts with stunning views, a good place to watch the migratory cranes and terns. The bar has a well-stocked cellar of imported French wines, champagnes, and German beers. The latter is all drawn from casks as cans despoil the environment.

Both the EuroDivers scuba school and the Maldives' base of the renowned Swiss Mistral windsurfing school have brand-new equipment and offer daily lessons for beginners at reasonable rates. Other activities include catamaran sailing, snorkelling, table tennis, volleyball and badminton.

Transfer: Two-and-a-half hours by wooden launch, $46.

Booking: M Shaazeewin, Fareedhee Magu, Malé: Tel. 32–3758; fax 32–8842. Resort: Tel. 44–1905; fax 44–1906; tlx. 77121.

## LESS THAN US$80

■ HELENGELI

The most northerly of all the resorts in North Malé Atoll, Helengeli is small with just 60 beds and basic salt-water showers. Amenities are simple and groups of divers not looking for any frills adore this island, and the swapping of their daring stories in the evening more than makes up for any lack of sophistication. The island has an excellent house reef and isn't visited much in comparison with other resorts' reefs. The diving is very good indeed with lots of big fish.

Transfer: 51 kilometres (32 miles) from the airport, $30 by *dhoni*.

Booking: Helengeli Reservation Office, Marine Drive, Malé: Tel. 32–5587; fax. 32–5625. Resort: Tel. & fax. 44-4615.

### ■ LANKANFINOLHU

A resort is currently being upgraded and will reopen August 1993 with 150 beds, and promises to be very impressive. It is a secluded island with a small but sandy lagoon, It is a good diving location.

Transfer:    Ten kilometres (six miles) from the airport, $20.

Booking:    Diza Travel & Trade, Malé: Tel. 32–3186, 2754; fax. 32–2754; tlx. 66088 LANFIN MF. Resort: Tel. 44–4576, 4582, 3597.

### ■ MEERUFENFUSHI

One of North Malé Atoll's largest islands—some 28 hectares (70 acres) in size—and the most easterly resort, Meerufenfushi takes three-quarters of an hour to walk around and is very beautiful. The name means 'sweetwater island', a bit of a misnomer, but it does have a beautiful wide lagoon. There is presently some speculation over whether this idyllic retreat may become a suburb of Malé over the next few years, despite its easterly location. Its 174 beds are popular with large groups, mainly Swedish, German, and British.

The bungalows are laid out in three different sections so that all the rooms have private verandas. The two restaurants' Maldivian chef serves European and Chinese food with occasional barbecues and wonderful lobster. The Sail and Surf School has three instructors who run PADI courses, and the big lagoon is ideal for water sports and snorkelling. Disco and all other amenities.

Transfer:    Three hours by boat, or 45 minutes by speedboat. $25 return trip.

Booking:    Champa Trade and Travels, Malé: Tel. 32–6545; fax. 32–6544; tlx. 66140. Resort: Tel. 44–3157; fax. 44–5946; tlx. 77002 CHAMPA MF.

### ■ ZIYAARAIYFUSHI

This mid-range resort on the far western side of the atoll recently doubled in size to 130 beds. The island itself is unspectacular with fewer palm trees than most resorts which makes the bungalows higher than anything else on the island. It makes up for this with a wider range of watersports than most resorts and a well-equipped diving school. Visitors rate its friendly atmosphere to be one of the main attractions of the place. As the cheaper resorts go, Ziyaaraiyfushi represents good value for money.

Transfer:    40 kilometres (25 miles) from the airport, $40 by *dhoni*.

Booking:    Phoenix Hotels and Resorts, Fasmeeru, Marine Drive, Malé: Tel. 32– 3181, 3587; fax. 32–5499; tlx. 66107 HORIZON MF. Resort: Tel. 44–3088; fax. 44–1910; tlx. 66146.

# South Malé Atoll

## US$220 +

### ■ COCOA ISLAND

My first impression of the tiny island of Makunufushi, from the deck of a *dhoni*, was of a graceful, barefooted figure walking towards me clad in designer hessian. Cocoa is a dream island run like a private club, a 16-bed exclusive bolt-hole for those for whom luxurious seclusion is as important as the glorious suntan, the unlimited water sports, glassy smooth sea and pristine natural beauty to be found elsewhere in the Maldives.

Tucked in amidst the bougainvillea and linked by sandy pathways, the island's eight A-frame cottages are havens of primitive aestheticism with a very Mediterranean or Polynesian feel. All the buildings rely on indigenous materials— rough, whitewashed, textured coral walls, palm wood beams, palm leaf thatch and lacquered satta ceilings—and blend harmoniously with their surroundings. Inside, the 'floor' is smooth sand which feels like silk to walk on, another unusual and inspired touch. Wooden stairs lead up to a loft where the bed is draped with a large mosquito net. Each of the cottages is designed to accommodate two or three persons, and sits right on the beach. Despite the deliberate omission of airconditioning, the rooms remain cool inside. All bathroom units are equipped with shower, toilet and 220V electrical outlets.

The impressively stocked bar sits on stilts above the lagoon, and is connected to the beach by a boardwalk. The restaurant produces high-quality meals for a small number of people, with the emphasis on fish specialities.

Cocoa's great advantage is its water sports facilities. The shallow, sheltered lagoon with its sandy bottom offers ideal conditions for sailing, windsurfing, and water-skiing. A nearby sandbank almost a kilometre (half a mile) long is perfect for those wishing to bathe or tan in seclusion. On the north side of the island, 30 metres (66 feet) from the water's edge, is a coral reef which drops off into the depths of the ocean, perfect for snorkelling.

Transfer:   40 kilometres (25 miles) from the airport, two hours by *dhoni* or 45 minutes by speedboat.

Booking:   M Gulisthaanuge, Fiyaathoshi Magu, Malé: Tel. & fax. 32–2326. Resort: Tel. 44–3713; fax. 44–1919; tlx. 77037 COCOA MF.

■ EMBUDHU FINOLHU

Embudhu Finolhu, a resort under Australian management, is currently being upgraded. It is a narrow island at the northern end of the atoll close to Malé. Its 20 deluxe, airconditioned rooms stand on stilts over the water, each with its own balcony and steps leading down to the water. The lagoon is sandy and a full range of water sports is offered. A small boat has been sunk just off the lagoon, allowing beginner divers the experience of diving amongst a wreck. Island-hopping, catamaran sailing, windsurfing and diving are amongst the water sports available.

Transfer:   Eight kilometres (five miles) from the airport, 35 minutes by *dhoni*, $20.

Booking:   G Makhumaage, Malé: Tel. 32–6483; fax. 32–2634. Resort: Tel. 44–4451; fax. 44–5925; tlx. 66081.

■ OLHUVELI VIEW HOTEL

This resort was opened 23 July 1992. It has 125 rooms, 30 of which are floating suites. In all rooms, there is fresh water, a television, in-house video and a minibar. Karaoke and a look-out tower (good for photography) are among the entertainments, as well as the usual water sports facilities, and a good deep sea fishing boat. One activity here that is unique in the Maldives is mini-golf.

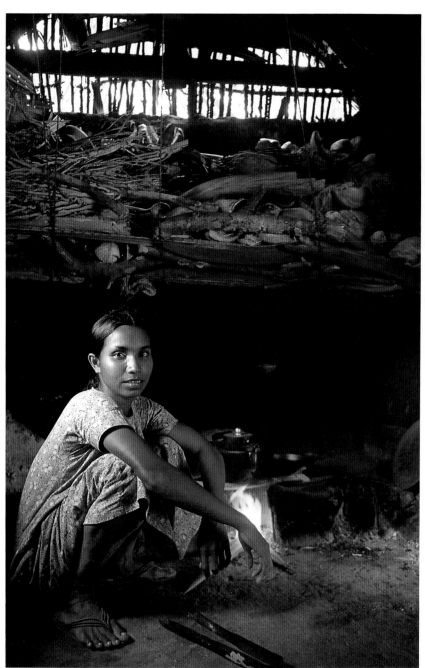
*Culinary preparations in a local kitchen*

Booking:   C/o Hunter Maldives, Chandanee Magu, Malé: Tel. 32–4952;
           fax. 32–3484. Resort: Tel. 44–2788; fax. 44–5942; tlx. 66224.

## ■ RIHIVELI

Opened in 1983, it certainly belongs in the 'very special' category. The 89-bed resort is run in a very personalized, idiosyncratic style with 12 French staff and 70 locals. Rihiveli, meaning 'silver sands', attracts mainly French visitors with smaller numbers of discerning Australians, Italians, Germans and British. One of its manager's quirks: groups (as opposed to individuals) of Japanese or Germans are not encouraged as a rule.

There are 36 cottages, each very spacious with aesthetic natural-fibre furnishings, in beautifully landscaped seclusion. Named rather than numbered, they are widely scattered over the island to ensure privacy. Each has its own hammock nearby, a nice languid touch. The restaurant is built over the sea with a *dhoni*-style servery. The view is remarkable and the food marvellous, mainly French and Italian dishes, with plenty of fresh fish, fruit and salads, and Maldivian buffets once a week. A good selection of wine and beer is stocked. Those who return four times are awarded their own wooden chair etched with their name beneath the leafy trees in the open-air, sand-swirled bar, guarded by a trio of parrots. Local dance and drum music figures in the weekly island programme and you can take tea and coconut flesh with the Maldivian staff every evening in the staff restaurant.

Rihiveli also scores highly for its amenities and activities. Free windsurfing, snorkelling, day and night-fishing, volleyball and tennis are offered year-round. Yoga and aerobics classes are held every evening in the open-air gymnasium. You can hire a catamaran, or go water-skiing and parasailing at a reasonable rate. You can also go trawling for deep-sea fish, or fish the local way with a hand line.

Diving enthusiasts rate Rihiveli's Eurodivers school highly for the emphasis placed on personalized tuition where classes are never for more than six people. PADI courses are offered for both beginners and advanced divers, and both day and night trips can be arranged. The Scuba-Pro equipment is top-class.

A converted *dhoni*, the Shadas, is moored here. It can be booked for simple day excursions or longer safari cruises at $480 per day for six people inclusive. A free three-day cruise on Shadas around South Malé Atoll can be applied for during the low season between 1 April and 30 October. Excursions and barbecues can be arranged on three tiny deserted islands close to Rihveli, easily reached by wading through the powder-soft sandy lagoon. You can also hire motorized *dhoni*s and speedboats. Excursions from Rihiveli include trips to local fishing villages, other tourist islands, and a full-day picnic off-island. Guradoo, a local fishing village with a population of 800, is 45 minutes away by *dhoni*. Felidhu, the island of birds, is about two hours away.

Transfer:    40 kilometres (25 miles) from the airport.
Booking:    C/o Imad's Agencies, Jawahiriyya, Chandhani Magu, Malé:
            Tel. 32–3441; fax. 32–6924; tlx. 66038. Resort: Tel. 44–3731;
            tlx. 66072 PITTMAT MF.

# US$150–220

■ DHIGUFINOLHU

The name literally means 'long island', an apt description of this sandbank that's 100 metres (328 feet) long and 60 metres (196 feet) wide, and low on palms and much vegetation. Fifty semi-detached bungalows, all airconditioned have the standard minibar and bath and shower with hot and cold, desalinated water. There are weekly buffets of local dishes under a German chef, two bars, weekly disco, board games, and late-night coffee shop. Popular with German, British and Japanese tourists who rate its informal atmosphere highly. Locals from neighbouring Guli come over once a week to do the inevitable *bodu beru*. Dhigufinolhu is joined to Veligandu Huraa by a 200 metre (220 yards) walkway. Facilities are shared between the two resorts, including the deserted island Boduhara.

Transfer:    19 kilometres (12 miles) from the airport, $35 return by *dhoni*.
Booking:    Dhigufinolhu Malé Office, Orchid Higun, Malé: Tel. 32–7058.
            Resort: Tel. 44–3611; fax. 44–3886; tlx. 77006 PALMTRI MF.

■ VAADHU

It's easy to see why this small and lush resort appeals to a large Japanese clientele. Here you can eat room-service sushi, clinch a business deal on the telephone to Osaka, and gaze out across the wide blue ocean.

There are three styles of accommodation in this 80-bed resort, each quite different. Top of the line are seven thatched 'Floating Cottages', impressively luxurious structures built on stilts over the lagoon and connected by wooden walkways. Inside, a glass floor gives you the impression of being in your own aquarium. At night, the blue of the sea is lit by soft lights and tropical fish appear to swim around on your floor. High-tech facilities include an IDD telephone in every room, even the bathroom. Two suites sleeping four, in two bedrooms, are particularly gorgeous; the other five cottages sleep two, in twin beds. Every cottage has a private balcony.

The other 24 rooms  are grouped in a small, airconditioned block called the 'Sunrise Wing'. The main difference is that they are not as private, romantic or delightful as the stilt cottages, despite their freshwater showers. All rooms offer the chance to take all meals by room service if you choose, a service popular with Japanese newly-weds.

There are two relaxed, open-air beach bars with sand underfoot. There are set menus of continental, Japanese, Chinese or French-Italian food, plus a weekly Maldivian buffet. The Japanese specialities include sushi, miso soup, and excellent tuna sashimi.

Vaadhu's location just off the channel separating North and South Malé Atolls, offers a rich variety of marine life. Nearby waters boast dolphins; sharks of various kinds including whale sharks; eagle and manta rays; and thousands of spectacular coral reef fish. It has its own diving centre with instructors offering training for both NAUI and PADI courses. Vaadhu is an excellent diving island with 14 of the best diving spots. Other activities include excursions in a glass-bottomed boat, day and night-fishing, use of a catamaran, water-skiing and scootering, and snorkelling.

Transfer: 15 minutes by speedboat, $15 return.

Booking: Henveiruge, Medhuziyaaraiy Magu, Malé: Tel. 32–5844; fax. 32–5846. Resort: Tel. 44–3976; fax. 44–3397; tlx. 77016 VADOO MF.

■ VELASSARU—LAGUNA BEACH

This resort has been given a face-lift to make full use of its broad beach of soft sand, and is one of the most beautiful in the archipelago. The 100 rooms are all airconditioned, arranged either as bungalows or in 28 double-storeyed groups. Rooms boast a minibar, hot and cold, desalinated water, a hair dryer, piped music, and IDD telephone. The three restaurants serve the usual range of cuisines including Italian food, and there's a gym and games room, swimming pool and tennis court. There is superb diving on the Vaadhu Channel and the well-equipped dive school, run by InterAqua, operates beginners' courses; windsurfing and parasailing instruction is also available. Excursions in a glass-bottomed boat, night sailing and fishing, and deep sea fishing can be arranged.

Transfer: 11 kilometres (seven miles) from the airport, $25 and 30 minutes by *dhoni*.

Booking: Universal Enterprises, 38 Orchid Magu, Malé: Tel. 32–2971, 3080, 3512; fax. 32–2678; tlx. 66024 UNIENT MF. Resort: Tel. 44–3042; fax. 44–3041.

■ VELIGANDU HURAA⁴

Another newish resort and quite secluded, 'Palm Tree Island' has just 16 rooms, all terraced and under thatched roofs, airconditioned with fans, with *en suite* bathrooms with showers and hot and cold, desalinated water. The lagoon is wide and clear. The sands are brushed off every night; the resturant is open to the air with a bar over the water. Veligandu Huraa is joined by a 200 metre (220 yards) wooden walkway to the

# An Honoured Guest

The one and twentieth of June, wee passed the Equinoctiall toward the North Pole. The second of July in the night, wee were miserably ship-wrackt upon the Bankes of the Maldives. The Inhabitants ledde us all together into a House in the middest of the Ile, where they gave us Fruits, Cocos, and Limons. Then the Governour of the Ile came to us called Ibrahim, who seemed very aged, he could speake some words of Portuguise, by the meanes whereof he asked us many things: after his people rifled us, and tooke away all that wee brought, saying that it did belong unto the King. Having beene in this Lodging the space of a day, they tooke the Master of our Ship with two Marriners, and convayed them to the King fortie leagues distant in the Iland of Male. The King sent his Brother in law with many Souldiers to our ship-wrackt Vessell, to get what they could.

The Kings Brother in law when hee went away, ledde me and two others into the Iland of Paindoüe, where at our first comming the Inhabitants gave us a little food, but when they saw that our companions had money (this money was about five hundred Crownes, which we tooke while wee were in the ship, and the first night we came on Land we buryed in the ground, which they after digged up wanting necessaries, but wee that were in the Ile of Paindoüe had none of it) they tryed by extremitie of famine to make us to give them some also, for they beleeved we had some. By reason of this evill resolution of the Ilanders to give us nothing without money, wee were brought into great miserie. All that wee could doe, was to gather Periwinckles on the Sea shoare to eate, and sometimes to meet with a dead Fish. This extremitie endured a long time, till that the Inhabitants seeing wee had no money, began to have a little more commiseration on us; we offered our service to them, to doe what they would imploy us about.

I went often with them to the neighbouring Ilands to get Cocos, and sometimes on Fishing, and in recompence of my labour they gave me part of the Fish or Cocos. While wee lived thus, I endeavoured my selfe to learne *the Language, which my companions despised. The Commander of the Ile seeing mee so studious of the Language, began to esteeme and favour me. Then there came one called Assaul Ocaounas Calogue, a Grand Signior; and because hee saw I could expresse my selfe in their Language, and daily studied to learne it, hee tooke me with him to carrie me to the King.*

*When wee arrived at Male, hee went presently to the King to render him an account of the Voyage, and among other things failed not to speake of mee to him. In the evening I went into a Court, whither the King was come to see that which was brought from our Ship. I saluted him in the Language, and after the fashion of the Countrey, which pleased him, and gave him occasion to enquire much concerning those things which were brought from the Ship: hee commanded the Signior that brought me, to lodge and entertaine me. The day following, I was busied with relating to the King, the manners and fashions of our people of Europe and of France. Hee made me see the Queenes, who imployed me divers dayes in giving answers to that which they asked me; being curious to understand the Habits, Manners, Marriages, and fashion of our French Dames.*

*I was about foure or five moneths in good health, and wanted nothing but the exercise of my Religion and my libertie, having all things else to my content. After this, I fell sicke of a hot burning Feaver. There passed not a day but the King and Queenes sent to know how I did, and every houre sent mee delicious viands to eate, and thus I continued a great while. Afterward the King gave me a lodging neere him, and every day rise out of his owne house, and necessarie provisions for my sustenance, hee gave me also a servant and money, and other presents, so that I became somewhat wealthy after the manner of the Countrey.*

*François Pyrard de Laval,*
Hakluytus Posthumus or Purchas His Pilgrimes, *1905*

slightly busier island of Dhigufinolhu, so you can share facilities. Or you can walk over to the uninhabited island of Boduhura. Island hopping and excursions to Malé and nearby boat-building villages are arranged, or you can even rent your own sailing *dhoni* for a few hours. The PADI-oriented Aquanaut Diving School is on a nearby island called Bushi.

Transfer:   19 kilometres (12 miles) from the airport; 90 minutes by *dhoni* or 45 minutes by speedboat, $35.

Booking:   Veligandu Huraa Malé Office, Orchid Higun, Malé: Tel. 32–7058; tlx. 77006. Resort: Tel. 44–3882; fax. 44–3886.

# US$80–150

■ BIYADOO

Large at 25 acres and now four years old, this resort is owned by Prabalaji Enterprises, a respected Indian hotel chain. It has 96 airconditioned rooms in six two-storey, concrete blocks. The island has luxuriant undergrowth prettily landscaped with bougainvillea, and is a more handsome bigger brother to nearby Villivaru (also Taj-run). There's usually a wide mix of nationalities, mainly German, Austrian and British. Rooms are pleasant without being special—rattan matting, a large double bed, running hot and cold water and mini-refrigerator—all overlooking the sea. The restaurant is airconditioned. Other facilities include a video bar, clubhouse, a weekly barbecue, disco and indoor games. Dinners are a triple buffet of seafood in Maldivian, European and international styles, as well as great curries. The great plus is the resort's own hydroponic garden, where they grow vegetables such as lettuce, tomatoes and cucumbers—quite unique in the Maldives where everything salad-like is flown in. The dive school is shared with Villivaru, see below.

Transfer:   29 kilometres (18 miles) from the airport, two-and-a-half hours by *dhoni*, $30.

Booking:   Prabalaji Enterprises, H Maarandhooge, Malé: Tel. 32–7014. Resort: Tel. 44–7171; fax. 44–7272; tlx. 77003.

■ BODUFINOLHU

Better known as 'Fun Island Resort', Bodufinolhu has a long, wooden jetty leading to the pier, which at night is floodlit to look like a long necklace across the sea. The island is actually very tiny, and is surrounded by a beautiful, sandy lagoon, perfect for snorkelling and swimming.

Opened in 1980 but upgraded in 1988, the resort's overall look and feel is modern and tasteful. The 88 rooms are in Maldivian-style thatched cottage buildings in blocks of two, three or four, all simple, whitewashed coral and concrete with lots of natural wood. Interiors sport Singaporean furnishings and all rooms have *en suite* bathrooms, hot and cold desalinated water, airconditioning, IDD dialing and a minibar. The resort is very popular with a mix of Italians, Germans, Japanese and Australians.

Food is of a high standard with Asian, Italian, Continental and Maldivian dishes; there is a good list of wines and champagnes, and the coffee shop has a wide à la carte selection.

The diving school offers PADI courses. Day tours roam as far as Embudhu Finolhu. Nearby is the Guraidhoo Channel and Banana Reef, an excellent spot for hammerhead sharks, manta rays, and whale sharks. Nearby are two uninhabited islands that can be reached at low tide, including a long thin strip of an island measuring only 30 by 800 metres (98 by 262 feet), beautifully shaded and relatively lushly vegetated. Watersports include snorkelling, water-skiing, windsurfing, and fishing.

Transfer:    39 kilometres (24 miles) from the airport, 40 minutes by speedboat, $50 return.

Booking:    Fun Island Resort,Villa Building, Ibrahim Hassan Didi Magu, PO Box 2073, Malé: Tel. 32–4478; fax. 32–7845; tlx. 66090. Resort: Tel. 44–4558; fax. 44–3958; tlx. 77099 FUNISLE MF.

■ BOLIFUSHI

A select, mid-priced resort with 32 chalets in two chalet-style blocks nestling on this very small island. All rooms have freshwater showers and are airconditioned. The lagoon is very beautiful and the whole atmosphere of this Shri Lankan-run resort is very service-oriented. Activities offered include diving, windsurfing, island hopping, a disco and volleyball.

Transfer:    14 kilometres (nine miles) from the airport, $25 by *dhoni*.

Booking:    Phoenix Hotels and Resorts Pte Ltd, Marine Drive, Malé: Tel. 32–5309; fax. 32–5499; tlx. 66107 HORIZON MF. Resort: Tel. 44–3517; fax. 44–5924; tlx. 66043 IOB MF.

■ EMBUDHU VILLAGE

The island is very pretty with a soft sandy beach and a wide lagoon. The atmosphere is very welcoming, the sort that works in a resort this size without seeming insincere. The Village's chief water sports attractions are the excellent snorkelling available on the house reef and the presence of the massive channel entrance nearby. This offers chances for widely different dives to Fusilier Reef to the north and a great drift dive down the channel itself, known locally as the 'Embudhu Express', where you can float past big fish, rays and sharks.

Transfer:    Eight kilometres (five miles) from the airport, 35 minutes by *dhoni*, $20.

Booking:    Kaimoo Hotels & Travel Services, Roanuge, Malé: Tel. 32–2212; tlx. 66035. Resort: Tel. 44–4776; fax. 44–2673; tlx. 66189.

### ■ VILLIVARU

This tiny 12-acre island is beautifully landscaped with palms and shrubs to provide the feeling of a primitive wilderness. It is a shame the beach is not one of the best in the Maldives. The resort has 24 naturally ventilated rooms with ceiling fans, and 36 rooms with airconditioning. Every room has a mini-refrigerator and a private veranda that opens onto the beach. The circular bungalows have satta-weave interiors, complimentary bathrobes and a good atmosphere.

There is an airconditioned à la carte restaurant, bar with video screen, club house, weekly barbecue, disco, and indoor games' facilities. There is fresh bread daily; the bar stocks Moet & Chandon and draft Warsteiner beer.

Both of the Prabalaji Enterprises resorts—Villivaru and Biyadoo—share a fully equipped diving school, the Nautico Watersports Centre, offering CMAS, VDTL, and PADI courses. More than half of the guests, most of whom are German, go diving during their stay. Special arrangements can be made for night cruises and night diving, picnics and excursions to other islands, or tours of the reef in a glass-bottomed boat. Daily boat trips (half a day or longer) visit an array of around 40 dive sites making full use of the nine channel openings in the vicinity. Major renovations are planned.

Transfer:    29 kilometres (18 miles) from the airport, two-and-a-half hours by *dhoni*, $30.

Booking:    Prabalaji Enterprises, H Maarandhooge, Malé: Tel. 32–7014. Resort: Tel. 44–7070; fax. 44–3742; tlx.77003.

## Below US$80

### ■ FIHA LLOHI

A budget resort at the southwestern tip of South Malé Atoll. The 78 rooms are situated a few metres from the water's edge. In addition to a shop, coffee shop, restaurant and disco, excursions are arranged and facilities are available for fishing, diving and volleyball.

Transfer:    45 kilometres (28 miles) from the airport, two-and-a-half hours and $30 by *dhoni*.

Booking:    Dhirham Ltd, Faamudheyri Magu, Malé: Tel. 32–3369; fax. 32–4752; tlx. 66027 DHIRHAM MF. Resort: Tel. 44–2903; fax. 44–3803; tlx. 66065 LHOHI MF.

*Religious devotion in Malé (above);*
*and in Tuamalaku (below)*

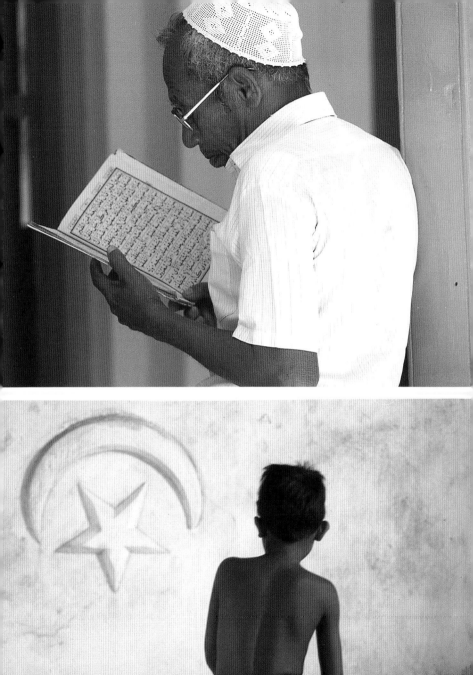

■ KANDOOMA

A popular resort, opened in 1985, patronized almost exclusively by Germans. If you don't have great expectations or are on a tight budget, this is an acceptable low-price option, appealing to the young-at-heart. It has 49 rooms, including 20 individual airconditioned bungalows. The restaurant offers a bland set menu plus Maldivian and German-style buffets. There is a coffee shop and a small seafront bar over the water. Facilities include table tennis, football, tennis and a dive school.

Transfer:   27 kilometres (17 miles) from the airport, three hours by *dhoni*, $25.
Booking:   M Zebey, Orchid Magu, Malé: Tel. 32–3360; fax. 32–6880. Resort: Tel. 44–4452; fax. 44–5948; tlx. 77073 KANDOO MF.

■ RANNALHI

This resort is very pretty, with lots of tall palm trees, a wide lagoon and soft sands; tranquil, natural and not too chic. The over-water coffee shop-cum-bar is now completed, the main restaurant has been refurbished, and a major restyling is underway of all the cottages, which previously were without airconditioning and had only cold showers. There's an excellent dive base but other water sports are not a priority here. One of the better resorts in the archipelago. Upgrading of facilities is currently taking place.

Transfer:   37 kilometres (23 miles) from the airport, about 31/2 hours by *dhoni*, $30.
Booking:   Jetan Travel Services, 55 Marine Drive, Malé: Tel. 32–3323; fax. 32–4628; tlx. 66086 JETAN MF. Resort: Tel. 44–2688.

# Ari Atoll

Many of the islands of Ari Atoll cannot be reached in the evenings. Boats and helicopters to the resorts do not travel at night, so if you do arrive in the evening, be aware that you may have to spend your first night in Malé. Similarly, if you have an early morning departure, your last night may also have to be spent in Malé.

## US$220 AND ABOVE

■ MADOOGALI

This resort has 50 rooms, mostly in the form of double cottages. The clientele is mainly Italian, so there are nine Italian staff. Most rooms are twin-bedded, airconditioned, tiled, and furnished with cane furniture, a bit spartan beneath the A-frame and thatched roofs, and there are no telephones. Seven larger 'special' rooms are under construction.

The open-air restaurant serves Italian and Maldivian food with evening waiter service. Breakfast and lunch are buffets. The bar has an interior garden looking out to sea over the small lagoon and a bright pastel colour scheme, a bit kitsch in this setting. Special Doctors Clinic available. Amenities include windsurfing, catamaran sailing, table tennis and badminton. The dive school offers PADI, CMAS and VIT accreditation.

Transfer: 78 kilometres (49 miles) from airport. Forty minutes by speedboat for $100. Two-and-a-half hours by *dhoni*. $250 round trip by helicopter.

Booking: Madoogali Malé Office, Marine Drive, Malé: Tel. 32–3222; fax. 32–7442; tlx. 66196. Resort: Tel. 45–0581; fax. 45–0554; tlx. 66126 MADUGAL MF.

### ■ NIKA

Nika is the designer fantasy of an Italian architect-turned-vagabond, Giovanni Borgo, who leased the island and built his first bungalow to live like a tropical prince in the early 1980s. He later added several more to turn his Robinson Crusoe island into a quiet hotel. The resort is named after the rare banyan *nika* tree that stands in the middle of the island.

More than 300 tons of soil have been imported from Shri Lanka, and the island is the best vegetated in the archipelago, especially noted for its large trees. Papayas, mangosteens, mangoes, watermelons, salad vegetables, and bananas, are all grown here—and ten gardeners are employed just to pick up all the leaves.

Nika sets its clocks two hours ahead of Malé, a common trick in the Maldives so that guests can feel utterly relaxed about leaving in time to catch their plane. Guests are given a plastic watch, set to 'Nika Time' when they arrive, which they can keep as a memento.

There are 25 bungalows, upgraded in 1987, and each is shaped to resemble a giant shell, built in a mixture of coral and whitewashed cement. Breadfruit leaf-imprints decorate the walls, the high ceilings are thatched and decorated with tortoiseshell, and the slatted wooden windows let in gentle breezes. Each bungalow has a small private beach and garden, large mosquito net, IDD telephone, and freshwater showers with hot water. The nicest bungalow suite is the Sultans' Bungalow with its old Shri Lankan furniture; the two bedrooms are ideal for a family. The restaurant is tastefully decorated with *lunghi*-style tablecloths and huge cowrie shells. The buffet-style food is excellent: fresh pasta, delicious cakes, and fresh fruit from the resort's own trees. There is a fine range of Italian wines and French champagnes.

# Ari Atoll

0    5    10    15 km

0         5         10 miles

*Reef*

Gangehi

Velidhu

Nika

*Indian*

*Ocean*

Madoogali

Maayafushi

Halaveli

Fesdu

Malhos

Thundufushi

Moofushi

Mandu

Machchafushi

Ranveli

Angaga

Mirihi

Kuda Rah

Diddhufinolhu

Veligandu

Kuramathi    Rasdu

Bathala

Ellaidu

Athuruga

*Indian*

*Ocean*

Omadu

*Reef*

Maafushivaru

N

*1000 m*

*1000 m*

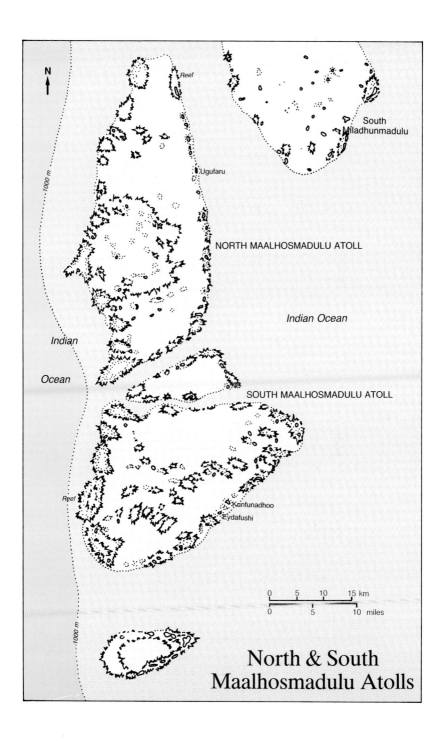

N

Reef

South
Miladhunmadulu

1000 m

Ugufaru

NORTH MAALHOSMADULU ATOLL

Indian Ocean

Indian

Ocean

SOUTH MAALHOSMADULU ATOLL

Reef

Kunfunadhoo
Eydafushi

1000 m

| 0 | 5 | 10 | 15 km |
| 0 | | 5 | 10 miles |

# North & South
# Maalhosmadulu Atolls

Nika is blessed with some superb diving spots, including the world-famous Fish Head Reef just two-and-a-half hours' away by boat, where you can expect to see eagle rays, stingrays and huge mantas, especially in February. There are also some non-aggressive white-tipped reef sharks. PADI progression courses up to Professional level are available. There's also a huge open-air aquarium which makes for fascinating viewing. It contains many nurse sharks, large turtles, stingrays, and many brightly coloured tropical fish that are fed every day on scraps from the resort's tables.

You can make excursions to the deserted island of Viamafaru, to Kuda Finolhu (literally, 'very small island'), and to Bodu Folhudhu, a nearby fishing village. Nika also has a jetty where yachts can moor overnight and a nice natural grass tennis court.

Transfer:  67 kilometres (42 miles) from Malé. Hummingbird Helicopters connects nearby Bodu Folhudhu with Singapore Airlines' weekly flight, followed by a 25-minute boat transfer, price $250; speedboat transfer from Malé takes about two hours, price $200.

Booking:  Book one year in advance for peak season; low season is less of a problem. Nika Hotel Office, 10 Fareedhee Magu, Malé: Tel. 32–5091; fax. 32–5097; tlx. 66124 NIKA MF. Resort: Tel. 45–0516; fax. 45–0577.

# US$150–220

■ GANGEHI

A beautifully landscaped wooden walkway encircles the island and is lit up at night to look like a string of fireflies ringing the island.

Opened in 1987, Gangehi has 25 rooms, eight of which are in the lagoon and whose balconies are perfect places to laze before taking a private swim. The others are set back in the vegetation and surrounded by bougainvillea. All rooms are furnished and decorated to a high standard, with *kunaar*-patterned bedcovers on black, wooden beds overlooking a spacious balcony, Thai cane chairs, black-tiled bathrooms with wood fittings, bidet and bathroom scales (a very Italian touch!), lots of mirrors, slats to provide private shade, thatched roofs, and Polynesian-style sliding doors.

The restaurant and bar are interconnected and look over the sea. The centrepiece of the tall thatched A-frame area is a giant aquarium in which lurks the poisonous Maldivian stonefish, a small shark, and many brilliantly coloured tropical fish. Simplicity is the order of the day, with design continuity, a décor of glazed terracotta pots, and fine tableware. There is also a resident pianist.

Gangehi is normally fully booked from December to May, almost entirely by

Italians, though some Germans and French also come. Only in the low season, during the European summer, is it relatively easy for individual tourists to book. The waters inside the large lagoon, however, are excellent for water sports or zipping about in the fleet of speedboats or canoes. Excursions to the uninhabited Mathiveri Finolhu, which actually belongs to Nika, can be arranged; honeymoon couples can be 'marooned' there for several hours in idyllic isolation.

Transfer:   70 kilometres (44 miles) from the airport.

Booking:   Holiday Club Maldives, H Sea Coast, Marine Drive, Malé: Tel. & fax. 32–3364; tlx. 66021. Resort: Tel. 45–0505; fax. 45–0506.

■ VELIDHU

A large island with accommodation for eighty people in 16 bungalows. Local staff predominate.

Transfer:   Six hours by *dhoni* or two hours by speedboat.

Booking:   Henveiru, Malé: Tel. 32–2149; fax. 32–4300; tlx. 66091 POLYCOM MF. Resort: Tel. & fax. 45–0595.

# US$80–150

■ BATHALA

A small resort on a very pretty island with a wide lagoon and soft sandy beach, it has 37 cottages with pointed roofs made of palm branches, each with a private walled garden and shower, and some with airconditioning. A good house reef offers fine diving opportunities for the well-equipped dive school.

Transfer:   57 kilometres (36 miles) from airport. $60 return by boat.

Booking:   Jetan Travel Services, 55 Marine Drive, Malé: Tel. 32–3323; fax. 32–4628; Tlx. 66086 JETAN MF. Resort: Tel. 45–0587; fax. 45–0558.

■ DIDDHUFINOLHU—ARI BEACH RESORT

This resort is approximately two-and-a-half hours by speedboat from Malé, or a short helicopter flight to the landing pad on the island. There are 76 airconditioned, linked bungalows, which have a freshwater shower, terrace and an IDD telephone. Facilities include a coffee shop, bar and souvenir shop, and for leisure, there is windsurfing, sailing, parasailing, tennis, badminton and fishing. This idyllic island is ringed with sandy beaches, and a free boat ride takes you to the coral gardens.

Transfer:   96 kilometres (60 miles) from the airport, three-and-a-half hours by speedboat.

Booking:   52 Marine Drive, Malé: Tel. 32–1930; fax. 32–7355; tlx. 66177. Resort: Tel. 45–0513; fax. 45–0512; tlx. 66178.

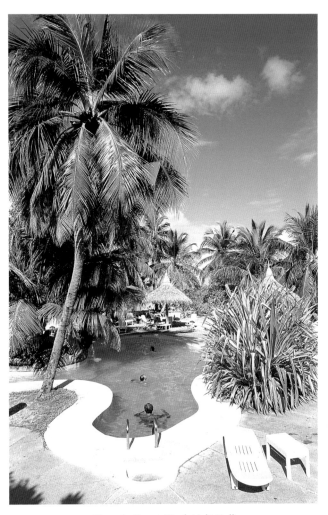

*Kurumba Resort, North Malé Atoll*

■ ELLAIDU

Sixteen bungalows on a small island means the atmosphere is simple and uncrowded in this mid-range resort that consistently scores high marks with its guests. The island itself is very pretty with a wide, sandy lagoon and a nice, sandy beach. Parts of the island are rather waterlogged, but the cottages, many of which are on stilts over the water, make the most of the setting. The management here seems to have got the right formula with a simple, intimate atmosphere and excellent food. The normal range of water sports and scuba opportunities are available.

Transfer: 57 kilometres (36 miles) from the airport, $50.

Booking: Safari Tours, 1 Chandhani Magu, Malé: Tel. 32–3524, 3760; fax. 32–2516; tlx. 66030 SAFARI MF. Resort: Tel. 45–0586; fax. 45–0514.

■ HALAVELI

A very attractive resort on a small circular island only 700 metres (765 yards) wide and reserved exclusively for the Italian tour operator, Grande Viaggi. Thirty-one simple bungalows and a circle of white sandy beach. The cook has five years' experience here. Scuba instruction given by three dive leaders; fishing and windsurfing facilities are also available. The facilities are presently being upgraded.

Transfer:  61 kilometres (38 miles) from airport. $60 return by speedboat.

Booking:  Eastinvest, Akiri, Marine Drive, Malé: Tel. 32–2719; fax. 32–3463; tlx. 77065. Resort: Tel. 45–0559; fax. 45–0564.

■ KURAMATHI

Two-and-half kilometres (one-and-a-half miles) long and just 600 metres (656 yards) wide, Kuramathi on Rasdu is one of a number of islands on which Buddhist relics have been discovered, a reminder of life in these far-flung places more than 1,000 years ago. Today it houses one of the most popular resorts in the southern half of the country (after a major upgrade in 1988). In fact, there are three categories of accommodation here, ranging from the straightforward to the exclusive, yet all sharing many amenities.

Laid out in the southeast corner is Kuramathi Village, 122 rooms, either singles or doubles, in round houses or in single-storey blocks. Popular with middle-class Germans, the village has its own diving school.

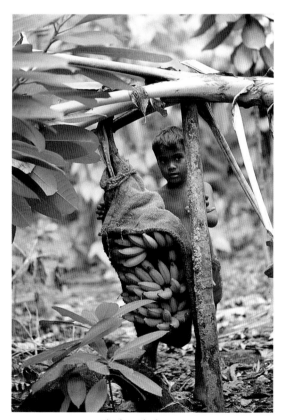

*Checking the harvest*

The second level of luxury is the Blue Lagoon on the 30-metre (33 yards) wide beach. All 50 rooms are airconditioned with their own minibar. Twenty are on stilts with ladders leading down to the water for swimming; double-bedded, tiled, fitted with cane furniture and telephone, they only lack a bath compared to the remaining 30 described below. This section is only a year or two old and appeals to the Swiss, Scandinavian, and Hong Kong clientele. The InterAqua Diving School is a German-Belgian concern.

At the top of the tree is the Kuramathi Cottage Club, 30 separate bungalows that are spacious and luxurious with their own clubhouse. The Cottage Club is popular with Italians on a par with Vabbinfaru and Giraavaru—exclusively so between December and May—and the diving school is, in fact, Italian-run.

The Club scores highly with its excellent food complete with imported pasta and herbs, a fine lunch and breakfast buffet, and choice of a set-menu dinner or buffet. The coffee shop has a sun-deck with soft sofas, open-air and chic. There's also a boutique. Expect club-style activities; windsurfing is included in the room price, part of which pays for the exclusive jetty. Night-fishing in a boat off-reef, Hobie-cats and parasailing are also available.

The shared amenities include a sports complex with a freshwater swimming pool, a gymnasium and a Chinese restaurant. Each section has its own disco, but the live band circulates. Excursions include a full day's sailing for a maximum of four people with a barbecue at the end of the trip, and visits to Rasdhu to see a local school, fishing village, and mosque. Diving spots include the Madivari coral garden.

Transfer:   48 kilometres (30 miles) from airport. One-and-a-half hours by speedboat, $30. Helicopter via Rasdhu, $97.

Booking:   Universal Enterprises, 38 Orchid Magu, Malé: Tel. 32–2971; fax. 32–2678; tlx. 66024 UNIENT MF. Resort: Tel. 45–0527; fax. 45–0556.

## ■ VELIGANDU

Pride of place in Veligandu on Rashu are the eight lovely suites along the water's edge with natural wood furnishings, Maldivian-style open-air bathrooms with sunken bathtub and adjacent telephone, and outdoor lights within a frangipani-filled garden. The balcony leads straight down into the sea. There are another 49 cottages, not quite so nice but still high quality, set back within the island. These are mainly twin rooms with some doubles; fresh hot and cold water, minibar, and all airconditioned. The resort attracts 80 per cent Italians and 20 per cent Swedes.

The atmosphere is very casual at the circular rattan-framed bar with sand underfoot and light cane chairs. The restaurant is similarly casual, and the food is reasonable without being exceptional.

The Crab Diving Centre offers PADI courses up to a maximum of eight pupils per class led by one to three instructors depending on the season.

Transfer: 48 kilometres (30 miles) from aiport. $60 round trip by *dhoni*.
Helicopter link via Rasdhu opening up this season.

Booking: Crown Company, Orchid Magu, Malé: Tel. 32–2432; fax. 32–4009; tlx. 66095 CROWN MF. Resort: Tel. 45–0594; fax. 45–0519.

## BELOW US$80

■ FESDU

A mid-range resort with 45 thatched cottages on a smallish island. Fesdu offers a friendly atmosphere in this secluded location right in the centre of the main atoll. There is excellent diving and the school is run by InterAqua. Upgrading is currently being carried out.

Transfer: 64 kilometres (40 miles) from the airport.

Booking: Universal Enterprises, 38 Orchid Magu, Malé: Tel. 32–2971, 3080, 3512; fax. 32–2678; tlx. 66024 UNIENT MF. Resort: Tel. 45–0541; fax. 45–0547.

■ MAAYAFUSHI

Part of a triangle of resorts run by Treasure Island, an Australian group. Here you use the Club Med-style bead-money system. Set menus in the restaurant offer simple food ('lobster available on request'); cabana-style bar. Sixty twin rooms with a few doubles in blocks of four, plus a handful of honeymoon suites.

Unlimited diving for one week listed as DM330; PADI lessons & CMAS accreditation are given by the resort's five instructors. Nearby is the famous Fish Head Reef. Night-diving, windsurfing, catamarans, and water-skiing, plus trips to nearby, uninhabited Magala island are offered. At present this resort is being upgraded.

Transfer: 61 kilometres (38 miles) from airport. $60 by *dhoni*.

Booking: H Morning Sun, Malé: Tel. & fax. 32–6658. Resort: Tel. 45–0588; fax. 45–0568; tlx 77124.

# Felidhu Atoll

## US$80–150

■ ALIMATHA

A gem of a resort with 50 rooms in separate huts in the middle of Felidhu Atoll, a sparsely populated group of islands south of South Malé Atoll with only two

(following pages) *Fun and games on the beach, Fuamalaku*

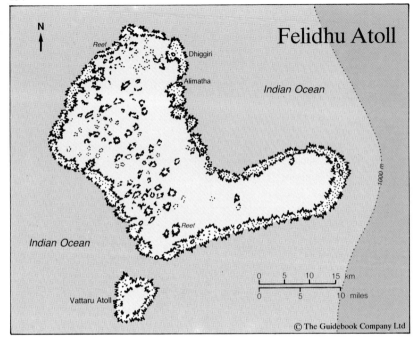

N

Reef
Dhiggiri
Alimatha

Felidhu Atoll

Indian Ocean

1000 m

Indian Ocean

Reef

Vattaru Atoll

| 0 | 5 | 10 | 15 | km |
| 0 | | 5 | | 10 | miles |

© The Guidebook Company Ltd

resorts—this one and nearby Dhiggiri. Extremely popular with Italian diving enthusiasts who visit both islands and the surrounding diving areas during the peak season, often with Club Vacanze. Food is an important attraction: the budget for meals is twice that of most other resorts. The management claims a repeat rate of 60 per cent after 12 years' operation. The impressive facilities include one of the country's two decompression chambers and an underwater photography school. Windsurfing is also offered.

    Transfer:   61 kilometres (38 miles) from the airport.

    Booking:   Safari Tours, 1 Chandhani Magu, Malé: Tel. 32–3524, 3760; fax. 32–2516; tlx. 66030 SAFARI MF. Resort: Tel. 45–0544; fax. 45–0575.

### ■ DHIGGIRI

This is a very special resort on a small round island, a partner to Alimatha, and Swiss-run under the aegis of its chief client, Manta Reisen. The 35 bungalows nestle in carefully secluded surroundings. The lagoon is particularly pleasant. All the usual amenities and facilities are on offer, including a dive school.

    Transfer:   59 kilometres (37 miles) from the airport.

    Booking:   Safari Tours, 1 Chandhani Magu, Malé: Tel. 32–3524, 3760; fax. 32–2516; tlx. 66030 SAFARI MF. Resort: Tel. & fax. 45–0592.

# Faadhippohu Atoll

## US$80–150

■ KUREDHDHU

The northernmost resort in the country, three times the size of the company's other resort at Veligandu, Kuredhdhu has 150 rooms with an open-air feel. However, its resources are not as sophisticated as those found in other resorts. Accommodation includes 15 family bungalows each containing three beds. All rooms have fresh hot and cold water but are without airconditioning, a relic of its former days when it was colloquially known as the 'Camping Resort' by the fraternity of divers that flocked here for the superlative waters. Swedish-managed, with several à la carte restaurants run by a Swedish chef, plus three coffee shops.

Excellent diving centre in a very remote area, and popular with Scandinavians and Germans. Pro-Divers, a Swedish organization, runs PADI courses with eight multilingual instructors from different countries. Three *dhoni*s go beyond the reef

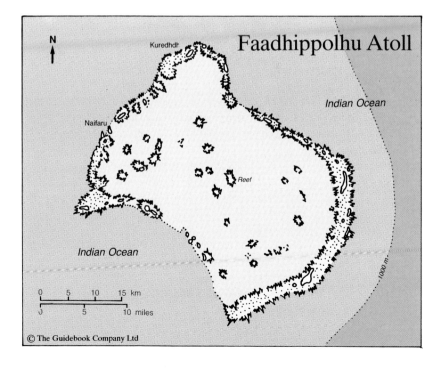

© The Guidebook Company Ltd

daily, so there are good opportunities for experienced divers to make the most of the impressive facilities.

Transfer:     128 kilometres (80 miles) to the airport.

Booking:     Champa Trade and Travels, Malé: Tel. 32–1751; fax. 32–6545;
              tlx. 66140. Resort: Tel. 23–0337; fax. 23–0332; tlx. 66201.

# New Resorts

The following resorts, located in Ari Atoll, started operating in the 1991–2 season, or very recently. There are plans for future development and this is the likely site of a lot more resorts once the transport problems are solved. Details available, at the time of going to press, are as follows:

## US$220 +

■ KUDARAH ISLAND RESORT

Each of the 30 individual rooms at this resort is airconditioned, with minibar and IDD telephone. As well as a disco, this resort has a fully equipped diving school, swimming pool, billiards, table tennis, volleyball, tennis court and gym. Excursions and fishing trips can also be arranged.

Booking:     2/F, H Merry Side, Marine Drive, Malé: Tel. & fax. 32–2335. Resort:
              Tel. 45–0550; fax. 45–0549; tlx. 66076.

## US$150–220

■ ATHURUGA ISLAND

This resort has 42 bungalows with hot and cold water and open showers. There are an open-air reception area, restaurant and bar. Sports facilities available include windsurfing, table tennis, volleyball, diving, excursions and night-fishing.

Booking:     Athuruga and Thundufushi Malé Office, Fareedhee Magu, Malé: Tel.
              & fax. 32–4435. Resort: Tel: 45–0508; fax. 45–0574; tlx. 77129.

■ MAAFUSHIVARU—TWIN ISLAND

On a small island with a pleasant beach, Maafushivaru has 32 airconditioned rooms with hot and cold freshwater showers. Diving, windsurfing, excursions and fishing are amongst the leisure activities.

Booking:     Universal Enterprises, 38 Orchid Magu, Tel. 32–2971; fax. 32–2678;
              tlx. 66024 UNIENT MF. Resort: Tel. 45–0524; fax. 45–0596

*Detail of lacquerware*

### ■ MIRIHI ISLAND RESORT

The island Mirihi is located 110 kilometres southwest of Malé. The resort has 30 double rooms over the water. Sports facilities available include windsurfing, sailing (top cat), diving, volleyball and table tennis. There is also a gym centre with a whirlpool.

> Booking:   Velangali, 2 Muiveyo Magu, Malé: Tel. 32–4910; fax. 32–4711; tlx. 66131. Resort: Tel. 45–0500; fax. 45–0501.

### ■ MOOFUSHI RESORT

Situated 94 kilometres from the airport, this resort has 60 bungalows, all with airconditioning, hot and cold water, and telephones. Sports facilities include diving, snorkelling, water-skiing, volleyball, gymnastics and excursions.

> Booking:   W.D.I. Private Ltd, 1/7 Marine Drive, Malé: Tel. & fax. 32–6433. Resort: Tel. 45–0517; fax. 45–0509; tlx. 66182.

### ■ THUNDUFUSHI ISLAND RESORT

Accommodation consists of 42 bungalows and there are also an Italian restaurant, bar and disco. A diving centre, water sports, excursions and fishing are available.

> Booking:   Athuruga and Thundufushi Malé Office, Fareedhee Magu, Malé: Tel.& fax. 32–4435. Resort: Tel. & fax. 45–0509.

# US$80–150

■ ANGAGA ISLAND RESORT

One of the newest resorts, Angaga is situated about three hours by speedboat from the airport. It is a tiny island surrounded by a sandy lagoon and crystal-clear water. The 50 spacious, airconditioned chalets are located just a few steps from the beach. A dive school and windsurfing are amongst the facilities available.

Booking:   Angaga Malé Office, Malé: Tel. 32–3706; fax. 32–6743. Resort: Tel. & fax. 45–0520; tlx. 66155.

■ ANGELS BEACH RESORT—MACHCHAFUSHI

This resort, opened in December 1992, has capacity for 100 guests, in airconditioned rooms with hot and cold water, minibar and IDD telephone. Facilities and services available are diving, windsurfing, water sports, volleyball, table tennis and tennis. There is also a disco.

Booking:   Nexus Trade and Travel Ltd, 57 Marine Drive Malé: Tel. 32–3121; fax. 31–1321; tlx. 66190.

■ RANGALIFINOLHU

At the time of going to press, 30 airconditioned rooms had been completed. Facilities include a coffee shop, main restaurant and shop. Diving, snorkelling, fishing and island excursions are available.

Booking:   Champa Trade & Travels, Malé: Tel. 32–6545; fax. 32–6544; tlx. 66140.

■ RANVELI BEACH RESORT—VILLINGILIVARU

This resort has 56 airconditioned, double rooms, each with hot and cold water, bathtub, IDD telephone and minibar. Leisure activities include volleyball, windsurfing, canoeing, island hopping, scuba diving, aerobics, snorkelling and fishing. There is also a swimming pool.

Booking:   Nexus Trade & Travel, 57 Marine Drive, Malé: Tel. 32–3121; fax. 31–1321; tlx. 66190. Resort: Tel. 45–0570; fax. 45–0523; tlx. 66207.

# Diving in the Maldives

The Maldives possesses some of the most spectacular dive spots in the world. For sheer diversity of the marine fish and invertebrates it is hard to beat. They also come big—mantas up to three or four metres (10–13 feet) and plankton-eating whale sharks much larger than that. Snorkellers, of course, can investigate only the upper levels of the water. But scuba divers—'scuba' stands for 'Self-Contained Underwater Breathing Apparatus'—can easily go down to 30 metres (98 feet), the legal limit for recreational dives in the Maldives. Beyond that depth, even though the water may be clear, the dangers of deep diving increase and render it off-limits to ordinary sport divers.

Decompression dives are illegal in the Maldives. This isn't so much of a problem as it might be as coral does not usually grow much deeper than 20 metres (66 feet). Most fishlife congregates around the coral reefs, so there is no need to go much deeper, except on a wreck dive. Drift-diving opportunities abound as ocean currents sweeping across from Indonesia towards Africa pass the tip of India and Shri Lanka, and surge through the Maldives, funnelled by the atolls down particular channels. Drift-dives make movement underwater easier and you do not need to use as much air or energy. The balancing danger is that unless you watch where you are going, you may be swept into coral heads.

## Qualifications and Instruction

Scuba diving has become something of an industry, with a central core of 200 instructors and more than 60 dive centres catering to the majority of the tourists. Most resorts have fully-equipped diving centres with well-maintained equipment and a staff of qualified instructors. The best have staff who have worked in the same resort for years, who know the local reefs like the back of their hand, and who are fluent in two or more European languages. Courses usually take four to five days to complete, though some may be shorter. Diving is a potentially hazardous sport that requires care and attention. As with any sport it is often the most experienced who take greater risks, and who consequently get caught in a potentially dangerous situation. Taking shortcuts is not necessarily a clever thing to do—or to be asked to do by an instructor—so make demands if he or she wants to rush you. Most dive schools operate the PADI certification system which is aimed at getting sport divers into the water quickly and enjoying themselves. If you want more training, check out the diving manuals of the BSAC, the most comprehensive of the lot. The main types

(clockwise) *Yellow crinoid (featherstar);
coral trout; lionfish on coral; moray eel*

of diving certification are as follows. (All but the last two are represented in the Maldives by one school or another).

**CMAS**—Confédération Mondiale des Activités Subaquatiques (French).
**PADI**—Professional Association of Diving Instructors (US).
**VIT**—Verband Internationaler Tauchschulen (German).
**Poseidon**—Poseidon Nimrod International Diving Club (German).
**Barracuda**—Barrakuda International Aquanautic Club (German).
**NAUI**—National Association of Underwater Instructors (US).
**BSAC**—British Sub-Aqua Club (UK).

All qualifications are accepted but PADI open water divers with less than 20 logged dives or other divers below 'BSAC sport diver' must dive with an instructor. You are cleared to 20 metres (65 feet) if you hold a European (CMAS, VIT, Poseidon) 2-star or PADI Open Water Certificate, and to 30 metres if you are a 3-star or Advanced Open Water diver.

Drift diving is being encouraged in some resorts because it is kinder on the reef, since the boat above follows the divers by trailing the flow of bubbles rising to the surface, instead of anchoring. (Repeated anchoring in the same area can cause a lot of damage to the coral.) Instructors will also watch out for those not paying attention as hordes of divers bumping into the reef can cause damage too.

The diving instructors will do everything possible to ensure your safety, but in case something does go wrong, the Maldives now has four decompression chambers in case of emergency: at Club Med and Bandos in North Malé Atoll, at Biyadoo in South Malé Atoll and at Alimatha in Felidhu Atoll.

If possible, you should take a medical certificate with you, but those without will be asked to sign a declaration of fitness to dive; and check your insurance.

# Approximate Water Sports' Costs—Guide Only

The following is an approximate guide to costs per person but please note that rates do vary from island to island, and from resort to resort:

|  | US$ |
|---|---|
| 1 day hire of snorkel, mask and flippers | 5.00 |
| 1 hour hire of windsurfer | 10.00 |
| 10 hours hire of windsurfer | 80.00 |
| 1 week unlimited windsurfing | 98.00 |

| Water-skiing—beginner's trial round | 15.00 |
|---|---|
| Water-skiing—advanced—per run | 15.00 |
| 1 scuba dive including equipment | 32.00 |
| 10 dive package including equipment | 280.00 |

Introductory diving courses are also available. There are other costs for unlimited diving, groups and those who bring their own equipment, who should only pay for tanks and weights.

## Dive Areas and Conditions

Most diving trips concentrate on North and South Malé Atolls, on Ari Atoll, and to a lesser extent Faadhippolhui and Felidhu Atolls. The water is warm and clear year-round, though with minor variations locally and seasonally. No wetsuit is necessary, though many people wear a thin suit until acclimatized to Maldive waters. Plankton blooming from mid-April can reduce visibility on the outer reef from about 40 metres (130 feet) down to about 20 metres (65 feet). The richest concentrations of plankton are usually on the eastern side of an atoll, which is where you will find the most fish. The northeast monsoon which arrives in January, brings clearer water to most parts of the atoll. In the clearest conditions you can see up to 70 metres (230 feet) below as you float over the reef edge. Tidal movements are also very important in determining visibility levels. Incoming tides bring clear water, outgoing ones carry sediment and thus can decrease visibility on the fringing reef and lagoon, and reef outlets nearby.

During the spells of rougher weather, usually in the southwest monsoon from May to October, the seas are often too rough to water-ski, and other water sports could also be restricted.

## Dangers

Coral reefs are not dangerous places, but there are some points you should bear in mind. Sharks can be seen regularly. Most sharks are not interested in humans, which are not their normal prey, unless provoked or cornered. However, if you see the 'threat display' (hunched back, nose up, pectoral fins down), it is wise to leave the scene. The most common types in the Maldives are the nurse, whitetip, reef blacktip, grey reef and silvertip sharks. Shark-feeding, an antic which made the Maldives famous, is not encouraged nowadays lest it change the habits of these predators which are, in any case, not always predictable. Barracuda are no danger to humans in clear water but could be a problem in murky waters. The moray eels have very sharp teeth, but the most fearsome-looking are sometimes the gentlest.

Ambush-predators can be a problem for the unwary who stumble onto the reef rather than just look at it, a good reason for diving neutrally buoyant. The scorpionfish has excellent camouflage and is poisonous. Stonefish and stingrays hide under the sand, so shuffle your feet as you move offshore to rouse them. Brightly coloured lionfish floating in mid-water should be avoided. Sea urchin's spines can cause nasty wounds. Fire coral gives a nasty sting, as can some cone shells that deliver a sharp dose of poison to divers who try to collect them.

# Some Favourite Dive Spots

In North Malé Atoll, near Girifushi, the Coral Garden and the Blue Lagoon is home to friendly eels and stingray. The area forms a protective bowl where many varieties of hard coral have formed themselves into a range of fantastic shapes, tall pillars and spreading fronds. Near Himmafushi there is Rainbow Reef and Devil Reef and near Lankanfinolhu is Manta Point, one of the most memorable dive sites in the archipelago, where a seasonal upswelling of plankton-rich water occurs between May and November at the reef's edge where it drops away to 2,000 metres (6,560 feet). Huge mantas come to the cleaning stations here, where they tolerate small groups of divers, and sometimes you can also see the giant whale shark. Manta Point is at its best July through October.

*Boat building in Thoddu (left);*
*turtles are easy to spot in the crystal waters (below)*

Kurumba has great coral formations at the Feydhu Caves. Nearby Bandos has Shark Point and Baracuda Giri, a diverse coral site with colourful crinoids, pinnacles of soft coral, and—naturally—barracuda. This is a good spot for photographing whitetip reef sharks and reef fish, like clown triggers and angelfish. Baros has a good close dive at Shallow Point while Giravaru has the Lion's Head, now denuded by shark-feeding visitors, but still a formidable outcrop next to the 200-metres (650-feet) deep Vaadhu Channel that runs between North and South Malé Atolls. The grey reef sharks here are about two metres (six-feet) long and are not interested in humans.

Near Malé is the Maldive Victory wreck dive, where a cargo vessel laden with whisky lies at 35 metres (115 feet) just off the end of the airport runway.

It went down in 1981 and is now well encrusted with marine life in its new surroundings. It sits upright on the bottom but is ripped by tidal currents, so divers have to fix lines from the dive boat to the masts.

In South Malé Atoll, Paradise Pass, which extends both sides of Vaddhu, offers some excellent dive sites including caves, a reef crest falling to around 30 metres (100 feet) and two channels with strong currents where incoming tides whisk you back to the house reef. Neighbouring Embudu has Fusilier Reef and the Embudu Wall which attract shoals of small fish which in turn attract skipjacks and yellow fin tuna, and even sailfish and marlin. The Embudu Express is the best drift dive in the Maldives, when winter monsoon currents combined with an incoming tide usher you on a two kilometre (over one mile) ride along the reef wall. Sometimes here you can hear the high-pitched squeaks and clicks of dolphins in the distance.

The dive sites of the Maldives have never been fully mapped, and the staff at any one resort can only hope to know a few dozen in the vicinity. Nonetheless, as more islands and atolls open up, the number of dive sites—already in the hundreds—will continue to grow. The opportunities for great diving can only get better, if that were possible!

# Dhivehi Glossary

| | | | |
|---|---|---|---|
| one | ekeh | Sunday | aaheeththe |
| two | dhey | Monday | hoama |
| three | thineh | Tuesday | angaara |
| four | hattareh | Wednesday | budha |
| five | fafeh | Thursday | buraasfathi |
| six | hayeh | Friday | hukura |
| seven | hatheh | Saturday | honihiru |
| eight | asheh | | |
| nine | nuvaeh | atoll | atolu |
| ten | dhihahe | island | dhu (or rah) |
| | | larger island | fushi |
| hello | assalamu alaekum | small island | finolhu |
| I, me | ahareng | small | kuda |
| you | kaley | big | bodu |
| him, her | eyna | round | va |
| how are you? | haalu kihine? | land | bin |
| very well | varah rangakhu | reef (or | |
| thank you | shukuriyiyaa | submerged coral) | faru |
| yes | aa | blue | noo |
| no | noon | dark blue | gadha noo |
| | | deep blue | madu noo |
| aiyah! | ekamakuvaa! | green | moodhu |
| what did you | | shallow | thila |
| expect? | kiku rani | turquoise | kula/vilu |
| how much is this? | mi kihaavarakah? | deep sea | kandu |
| expensive | vara agu bodu | coconut | kurumba |
| cheap | agu heyo | vegetables | tharukaree |
| today | miyadhu | fruit | meva |
| yesterday | iyee | rice | baiy |
| tomorrow | maadhamae | fish | mas |
| morning | hendhunu | turtle | vela |
| afternoon | mendhuru fas | shark | miaru |
| | | basking shark | faana |
| | | | nidhanmairu |

# Recommended Reading

Battuta, Ibn  *Travels in Asia and Africa* (London: Routledge Kegan Paul, 1983)

Bell, H C P  *The Maldive Islands: Monograph on the History, Archaeology and Epigraphy* (Colombo: Ceylon Government Press, 1940)

Burgess, C M  *The Living Crowries* (New York, London: 1970)

Eibl–Eibesfeldt, I  Trans. Gwynne Vevers,  *Land of a Thousand Atolls* (London: MacGibbon & Kee, 1965)

Gray, A  trans., assisted by H C P Bell  *The Voyage of Francois Pyrard de Laval to the East Indies, the Maldives, the Moluccas, and Brazil* (London: Hakluyt Society, 1888)

Hanna, N  *BMW Tropical Beach Handbook* (London: Fourth Estate, 1989)

Hass, H  *Expedition into the Unknown* (London: Hutchinson, 1965)

Heyerdahl, T  *The Maldive Mystery* (London: George Allen & Unwin, 1986)

Holiday, L  *Coral Reefs* (London: Salamander Books, 1989)

IUCN  Conservation Monitoring Centre *Coral Reefs of the World. Volume 2: Indian Ocean, Red Sea and Gulf* (Cambridge, UK; Gland, Switzerland; Nairobi, Kenya: IUCN/UNEP, 1988)

Maloney, C  *People of the Maldives Islands* (London: Longman, 1980)

Moresby, R  Indian *Navy Nautical Directions for the Maldive Islands & Chagos Archipelago* (1840)

Webb, PA  *Maldives: People and Environment* (Bangkok: Media Transasia, 1988)

Yajima, H, ed, *Islamic History of the Maldives: Hasan Taj-al-Din* (Tokyo: Institute for Study of Language and Culture of Africa and Arabia, 1982–4)

Admiralty maps of the Maldives can be bought in Alex Perreira's on York Street, Colombo, Shri Lanka. The East Indian Pilot, an Admiralty publication, also has details of the Maldives.

*Detail of the blue and white minaret*

# Index

(Following pages) *Surprisingly few islands are inhabited in this expanse of blue*